300

LESSONS
IN ART

Robert Henkes

J. Weston Walch, Publisher

Contents

To the Teacher ▬▬▬▬▬▬▬▬▬▬

This handbook, *300 Lessons in Art*, is a rich resource of creative art activities presented in a practical "planbook" format. Designed for use with junior and senior high school art classes, it will serve experienced and less experienced teachers alike as a valuable source of ideas and methods. Many of the lessons can be used in a single class period; and most require only inexpensive art materials.

Each activity is presented as an easy-to-use lesson plan. The plan not only indicates the level of student competency required, it also explains the lesson's purpose and outlines the necessary materials and procedure. Guidelines for evaluating student work are also a part of each plan. Many lessons are accompanied by helpful and inspiring photos of student work.

The 300 lessons can be used individually in whatever sequence you choose, but for convenient reference they are grouped into seven chapters. The projects within each chapter are related by general topic, but they differ in media, technique, composition, or purpose. The first chapter centers on drawing techniques and media, the second on painting techniques, composition, and ideas. The third chapter offers a variety of two-dimensional projects other than drawing and painting, and the fourth chapter focuses on three-dimensional projects.

The fifth chapter is designed as a testing facility, for a change of pace, for creative exploration, and/or for therapy. All seventy-five activities in this chapter are designed to be completed within a forty-five minute time period, but the results may be useful as preliminary sketches for long-range projects.

The sixth chapter deals with art appreciation by doing, and the seventh chapter is a collection of twenty-five miscellaneous art activities.

Some major kinds of art have not been included in this book because they require complicated procedures, expensive equipment and supplies, or both. Such experiences as etching, lithography, serigraphy, photography, ceramics (wheel), weaving (loom), jewelry, stained glass, and several textile projects can best be served through other resources.

We hope this widely varied collection of art lessons will stimulate you and your students, helping you to make the development of artistic expression challenging, interesting, and enjoyable.

J. Weston Walch, Publisher

CHAPTER I   DRAWING ▬▬▬▬▬▬▬▬▬▬

1. **Natural Texture Drawing**
2. **Inventive Texture Drawing**
3. **Contour Figure Drawing**
4. **Contour Drawing of Heads**
5. **Contour Drawing of Hands**
6. **Contour Drawing of Clothing**
7. **Contour Drawing of Figure and Background**
8. **Gesture Drawing of Stationary Objects**
9. **Gesture Drawing of Moving Objects**
10. **Triangular Drawing**
11. **Colored Chalk Drawing**
12. **Wet Chalk Drawing**
13. **Crayon Drawing**
14. **Realistic Optical Drawing**
15. **Abstract Symmetrical Optical Drawing**
16. **Abstract Nonsymmetrical Optical Drawing**
17. **Pop Drawing**
18. **Silhouette Drawing**
19. **Volume and Mass Drawing**
20. **Drawing of Deliberate Distortion**

LESSON 1   Natural Texture Drawing   Beginning/Intermediate/Advanced

Purpose: To encourage students to use textural patterns of nature in differentiating objects and space.

Materials: Pencils, white drawing paper, black fine-line felt markers.

Procedure: Have students examine natural objects: tree bark, corn leaves, rocks, insect wings, grass, pebbles—for their textural pattern qualities. Have students examine drawings of Tobey, Dubuffet, Graves, Moore, and others for textural patterns. Then have students make contour drawings of landscapes or objects. Consider contrasting patterns and textures appropriate for given forms. Have students fill in contour areas with textured patterns that coincide with the natural textures of the objects. After the composition is complete in pencil, students should carefully outline the drawing with black fine-line markers before the addition of textures.

Evaluation: Based on strong, natural textural patterns, contrast, and spatial relationships.

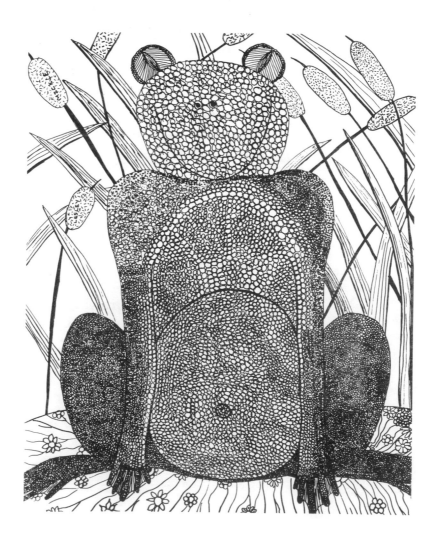

The Toad

Lesson 2 **Inventive Texture Drawing** **Beginning/Intermediate/Advanced**

Purpose: To encourage students to use their imaginative powers beyond the limits of academic portrayal.

Materials: Pencils, white drawing paper, black fine-line felt markers.

Procedure: Have students draw lightly in pencil a close-up view of a single aspect of nature: fish, frog, insect, leaf, piece of fruit, rock, ant, fly, beatle, etc. The drawing should be enlarged so that it occupies the entire paper. Any remaining space on the paper is considered as the object's environment. After completion of the drawing, the entire composition is carefully outlined with the fine-line black felt marker. Consideration is then given to the shapes within the object that are patterned into inventive textures such as circles, triangles, checkerboards, ovals, and lines. These too are outlined. Contrast is created by placing lines or shapes closely together for dark areas and farther apart for lighter areas. After the entire object or animal is outlined, have students attend to the background so that it too contrasts with the main idea. The simplicity of the background will depend on the complexity of the focal idea.

Evaluation: Based on imaginative portrayal, selection of inventive textures, and ultimate arrangement.

The Bird and Its Young

LESSON 3   **Contour Figure Drawing**   **Intermediate/Advanced**

Purpose: To eliminate stereotyped features of drawing by a closer visual contact with the human figure.

Materials: Pencils, white drawing paper, black felt markers.

Procedure: Select students to pose in front of class. Simple and plain clothing is desirable so that the focus is on the figure instead of incidentals. Have students focus their eyes on a particular spot on the model and place their pencils on an appropriate spot on the paper. The eye and the hand serve the same purpose. There should be complete coordination between the eye, the hand, and the mind. Encourage students to stop drawing at any time, but to draw only when the eye is on the model. Have students continue this stop-and-go method until the posed model is completely drawn. Complete coordination will prevail only after sustained and consistent practice.

Evaluation: Based on clarity of line, number of lines that connect at the proper points, and emotional content. Based also on eventual duplication of the figure to its nearest likeness.

LESSON 4   **Contour Drawing of Heads**   **Advanced**

Purpose: To continue the contour process into a selected aspect of the figure.

Materials: Pencils, white drawing paper, ball-point pens, black fine-line felt markers.

Procedure: Concentration becomes more intense. To enable emotional portrayal, have student models display different facial expressions as they pose. Again, have students unite the eye and hand as they draw first the head shape, then the inner and outer contours of the hair. Then have them appropriately position the pencil inside the already-drawn head and draw each eye separately, using the stop-go method. Expression of the nose and mouth follow.

Evaluation: Based on the honesty of line and detailed exhibit of the personality and emotional content of each pose, and, of course, the legitimate distortion that should exhibit itself within each pose. The convincing appearance of each contour drawing should always be considered.

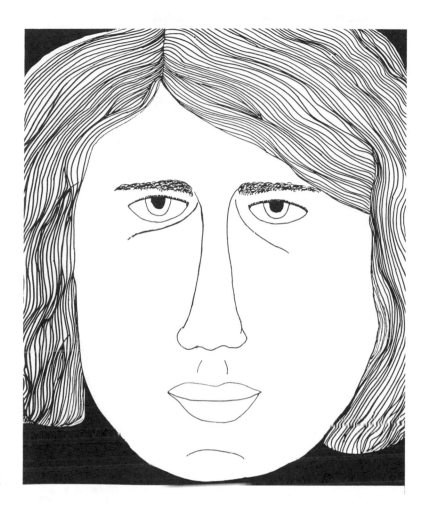

Portrait Head

LESSON 5   Contour Drawing of Hands   Intermediate/Advanced

Purpose: To expose the student to a closer relationship between himself or herself and the visual stimulus.

Materials: Pencils, white drawing paper, black felt markers.

Procedure: In order to more easily control the eye, mind, and hand coordination, have each student rest the left hand on the desk and draw with the right hand. Have students change position of the posed hand several times. The inside of the hand should be drawn first, then the outside. Remind students to observe fingernails, rings, and knuckles.

Evaluation: Based on realistic portrayal as well as the variety of poses expressed. There should be a marked improvement over the head and figure drawings because of the shorter distance existing between the student and the stimulus.

LESSON 6   **Contour Drawing of Clothing**   **Advanced**

Purpose: To express the importance of folds and creases in clothing in relation to the
                  human figure. To avoid rigid portrayal of the human form.

Materials: Pencils, white drawing paper, felt markers.

Procedure: Select various students to pose, each sporting a different type of clothing. Have
                  students draw only the torso, emphasizing the folds in the clothing. Remember,
                  each line begins from another line. Each type of clothing—cotton, silk, satin,
                  nylon, leather, and corduroy—will have different folds. The weight of the cloth-
                  ing will produce different folds, too. A good practice trick is altering the position
                  of one's own handkerchief or tissue several times and drawing the different posi-
                  tions.

Evaluation: Based on the convincing manner in which the folds are expressed and the obvi-
                  ous distinction between the different materials.

LESSON 7   **Contour Drawing of Figure and Background**   **Advanced**

Purpose: To develop and complete a total composition of figures and background. To
                  overlap the human form, suggesting the receding and advancing of the contour
                  method. And finally, to incorporate in contour fashion a background study ap-
                  propriate to the initial drawing.

Materials: Pencils, white drawing paper, felt markers, ball-point pens.

Procedure: Differing from the drawing of a single figure, a grouping of figures will demand
                  overlapping. Place posed models in various positions: sitting, standing, kneeling,
                  and lying, one in front of or behind the other. Students then select the entire
                  composition to draw, or only a segment of it. The larger the drawing, the less
                  need for a background. Particular difficulty may come up in overlapping. Suggest
                  to students that they draw more slowly so that the connection of lines between
                  one figure and another is more accurate.

Evaluation: Based on the completeness of portrayal, overall uniformity, clarity of line, and
                  emotional content.

LESSON 8   **Gesture Drawing of Stationary Objects**   **Advanced**

Purpose: To quicken the execution of a drawing in order to register only the essentials.

Materials: Pencils, white drawing paper, felt markers, ball-point pens, crayons, chalk.

Procedure: Set up a still life or a group of posed models. Have the students draw a complete composition in a period of 20 minutes. Then have the students draw the same composition in 10 minutes. Cut the time to 5 minutes, and finally to one minute. As the students draw, reinforce the importance of rapid drawing. Then continue one-minute drawings, changing the stimulus each time. Mention that time is short and that the drawing must be complete.

Evaluation: Based on the illusion of movement, accentuation of essential parts of the stimulus, and elimination of nonessentials.

LESSON 9   Gesture Drawing of Moving Objects   Advanced

Purpose: To record movement and eliminate all nonessentials. To express the movement and action of the stimulus.

Materials: Crayons, chalk, pencils, ball-point pens, felt markers.

Procedure: Have students pose in movement or action positions. Physical exercises, wrestling, marching, and cheerleading are examples. Have students draw the figures as they move. There is no time limit, just a continual process of drawing, recording the movement of the body. Students should work quickly, ignoring the details and being alert only to the greater movements.

Evaluation: The complete drawing should evidence such movement as swirling lines for wrestling, and choppy vertical and diagonal lines for marching and cheerleading.

LESSON 10   Triangular Drawing   Intermediate/Advanced

Purpose: To use a single geometric shape—in this case the triangle—in the organization of a complete composition; to use the triangle as a means of displaying recessive and three-dimensional qualities.

Materials: Black felt markers, ball-point pens, white drawing paper.

Procedure: Setting up a still life or a group of figures is desirable, but the student may prefer to express a mental image. First, have the student lightly sketch an idea to provide a starting point. After the sketch is complete, alterations of the drawing are made in the form of triangles. As the drawing develops in detail, no segment of the idea should be destroyed. The idea must always remain recognizable, even though it may appear abstract. In order to reform the significant idea, additional lines are drawn to form additional triangles. As more triangles are developed within a given area, the drawing begins to reveal a shading technique different from common methods. Remember, the smaller the triangles, the darker the area, and the larger the triangles, the lighter the area.

Evaluation: Based on the retention of the identity of the initial idea or composition, and on the reinforcement and strength evidenced in the triangular process of shading.

LESSON 11   **Colored Chalk Drawing**   Intermediate/Advanced

Purpose: To express freely an idea suited to the broad strong colors of chalk. To accomplish blending of color as a prerequisite to painting.

Materials: White drawing paper, colored chalk, pencil.

Procedure: Have students work from a visual stimulus. A still-life setup is ideal. Suggest that the entire setup need not be drawn. Enlarged segments may meet individual needs. The composition should be drawn with a light color on large white paper. After the composition is complete, areas should be shaded in with short broad strokes of the chalk. Students should blend colors wherever needed and be aware of necessary contrast. Textures may be added. Be sure the chosen still life fits the size of the paper so that little negative space remains. Fixative can be applied later to avoid chalk smudges.

Evaluation: Based on completeness of drawing, consistent contrasts, and textural qualities.

LESSON 12   **Wet Chalk Drawing**   Beginning/Intermediate/Advanced

Purpose: To use the wet-paper approach to formalize an all-over layout of color, and to incorporate the results with sharp detailed accents of dry chalk.

Materials: Large white drawing paper, sponge, brush, colored chalk.

Procedure: Have students draw an idea lightly with pencil onto white paper. The paper is then brushed or sponged with water. Before the wet paper reaches the damp stage, colored chalk is carefully applied, following the penciled-in lines of the drawing. As the colors spread beyond the lines, other colors are applied, blending into the first. If the paper dries out, it may be sponged again. Have the process continued until the entire drawing is colored.

As an added touch, have students reinforce the original drawings with dry chalk, using the sharp edges of the colors. Such accents sharpen a drawing. Be sure drawings are dry before doing this.

Evaluation: Based on the fullness of color blend and the accompanying accents.

LESSON 13   **Crayon Drawing**   Beginning/Intermediate/Advanced

Purpose: To blend colors to effect a three-dimensional appearance, and to use secondary colors extensively.

Materials: Pencil, crayons, white drawing paper.

Procedure: Have students draw with pencil onto white paper a figure composition of posed models or a still-life setup of fruits and flowers. Application of colors should blend and shade three-dimensional qualities. Consideration should also be given to recessive and advancing areas. Textural qualities become important as details are added. Have the students eliminate outlines, so that the original line drawing becomes a volume and mass expression.

The negative space surrounding the area is attended to by incorporating a second idea. In the case of the posed models, it should be a background of identification to the models. In the case of the still life, it should be a subdued color suggesting a wall or window. Finally, have students accent or highlight colors where needed.

Evaluation: Based on the strength of composition and the convincing manner in which areas recede and advance. Never underestimate the background. It can make or break composition.

LESSON 14 Realistic Optical Drawing   Advanced

Purpose: To cause an optical illusion within a realistic setting.

Materials: Pencils, white drawing paper, black fine-line felt markers.

Procedure: A pencil drawing stemming from mental images or visual stimuli (still life or posed figures), recording several areas or ideas, should be outlined completely with fine-line black felt markers. Then each adjacent area should be lined opposite to the direction of the shape or area. For example, if two rectangles are side by side, one is filled with horizontal parallel lines and the adjacent one with vertical parallel lines. The distance between the lines establishes darkness or lightness, contrasting the two adjacent shapes. If lines are drawn vertically or horizontally within two adjacent shapes, the optical effect can be secured by placing the lines further apart in one area and closer together in the other. As the process continues, students should be alert to opposing forces so that the optical illusion takes place. The drawing will remain realistic because lines are applied within the limits of each realistic shape, but the whole will appear optical.

Evaluation: Based on the retention of the original drawing in conjunction with the effects of optical illusion. (Photo on page 10.)

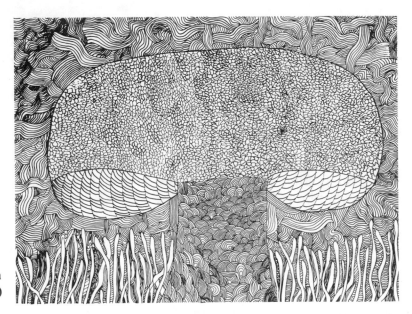

Mushroom
(Lesson 14)

LESSON 15   **Abstract Symmetrical Optical Drawing**   **Intermediate/Advanced**

Purpose: To create an optical illusion by using black and white geometric shapes to make an abstract pattern.

Materials: White drawing paper, pencil, rulers, felt markers.

Procedure: Have students locate the center of their drawing paper. Through the center point, several diagonal lines should be drawn. The more lines, the more complex the design. Then a rectangular shape is drawn equally distant from the center, using parallel lines. Additional rectangles, enlarged as they are drawn, should lead to a completely outlined drawing. The optical illusion emerges as opposite shapes are blackened into a checkerboard pattern.

Evaluation: Based on the complexity of design, neatness, and the optical-illusion effect.

LESSON 16   **Abstract Nonsymmetrical Optical Drawing**   **Advanced**

Purpose: To alter design as the pattern progresses, and to develop the ability to improvise.

Materials: White drawing paper, pencils, rulers, black fine-line felt markers.

Procedure: Have students simply crisscross lines in pencil across their drawing paper, then outline the pencil lines with black markers. Follow up by blackening in shapes so that a black shape is adjacent to a white shape. As the design progresses, it will become evident that two white sections will be side by side. An additional section must divide the two in order to continue the black-and-white sequence. This change of design will occur often, so the student must make changes until a perfect black-and-white sequence is achieved.

Evaluation: Based on the eventual excitement of design caused by the complexity and organization of the optical pattern.

LESSON 17   Pop Drawing   Intermediate/Advanced

Purpose: To incorporate commercial products into a complex composition of lettering, overlapping, contrast, and details.

Materials: Pencils, white drawing paper, rulers, gum and candy wrappers (or any commercial product advertisements), erasers.

Procedure: Have students gather several gum and candy wrappers. After selecting one, have them copy and enlarge it in detail. Select a second wrapper, and angle it into the first by overlapping. Again, copy in detail. This process is continued until 10 to 12 wrappers are drawn and shaded in detail, with all overlapping shown. Contrast is most important. Tones should range from white to black.

Evaluation: Based on the clarity and complexity of design, variety of shapes and sizes, sharpness of detail, and quality of letters.

LESSON 18   Silhouette Drawing   Intermediate/Advanced

Purpose: To equalize the distribution of negative and positive space in a realistic setting.

Materials: White drawing paper, pencils, black felt markers.

Procedure: In order to avoid stereotypes, dictate a limited number of objects to be drawn into a complete composition. Have students outline the objects with felt markers and blacken areas to be silhouetted. In order to keep overlapped objects separated, white lines should remain free. Since the objects drawn are positive, it will be simple for the silhouette to emerge, because the remaining space is negative and consequently will remain untouched. Remind students to be careful not to overwork, and to allow enough background so that the silhouette will benefit.

Evaluation: Based on completeness and proper unity between negative and positive (white and black) areas.   (Photo on page 12.)

Tenants
(Lesson 18)

LESSON 19   **Volume and Mass Drawing**   **Advanced**

Purpose: To reflect in pencil three-dimensional qualities on a two-dimensional surface.

Materials: Pencils, white drawing paper or newsprint, erasers.

Procedure: Suggest working from a still-life setup or a group of posed models. After students draw the complete composition in pencil, have them use the side of the pencil to shade each three-dimensional area from dark to light to dark. As the shading takes place, remind students to consider the composition as a whole, not just isolated parts. An added touch would be the application of textures, accents, and details. Contrasting areas should be evident without the use of outlines.

Evaluation: Based on the strength and solid appearance of the three-dimensional forms as well as the unity of the composition.

LESSON 20   **Drawing of Deliberate Distortion**   **Advanced**

Purpose: To distort purposely in order to understand reality, and to appreciate the reasons for exaggeration.

Materials: Pencils, white drawing paper, fine-line felt markers, crayons, chalk.

Procedure: Using 3 pieces of white drawing paper (9″ x 12″), have students fold 2 pieces lengthwise so they measure 4½″ x 12″. The third piece remains 9″ x 12″. On the 9″ x 12″ piece, have students draw a human head occupying most of the paper. On the 4½″ x 12″ paper, the same head is drawn 4½″ wide and 9″ tall. The third piece requires a head 9″ wide and 4½″ tall. This creates three heads—(normal, tall and narrow, and fat and short).

Now have students place the three heads in window frames of an apartment house. Each head should be drawn looking out of its own apartment window. The space surrounding the three window frames becomes a social commentary. The space should be transformed into wood siding, brick surface, or stone, in good condition or bad.

Finally, have students add emotional expressions to the three human faces. An idea or object located within the window frame should also indicate this emotional state.

The entire drawing should be outlined and textured with fine-line felt markers. If coloring, use chalk or crayon.

Evaluation: Based on the distinct difference shown in distorted faces, in addition to the social commentary connected with the apartment siding.

CHAPTER II   PAINTING ▬▬▬▬▬▬

21. **Defined Line Painting**
22. **Crayon Encaustic Painting**
23. **Close-up Tempera Painting**
24. **Faraway Tempera Painting**
25. **Word Painting**
26. **Two Sections of a Single Aspect of Nature**
27. **Three Sections of a Single Aspect of Nature**
28. **Multiplicity of Environments**
29. **Painting in Cool Colors**
30. **Painting in Warm Colors**
31. **Painting in Primary Colors**
32. **Painting in Tones of a Single Primary Color**
33. **Montage and Tempera Painting**
34. **Collage and Tempera Painting**
35. **Finger Painting**
36. **Tempera and Enamel Painting**
37. **Enamel Painting**
38. **Oil Painting**
39. **Mixed Media Painting**
40. **Mural Painting**

LESSON 21   **Defined Line Painting**   Intermediate/Advanced

Purpose: To introduce a method of watercolor combined with ink to show the relationship between line, form, and texture.

Materials: White drawing paper, tempera paint, brushes, water containers, black fine-line felt markers.

Procedure: Students draw lightly in pencil on white paper a vase of flowers or similar stimuli. The paper is wetted with brush or sponge. Have students apply a brushful of paint to the wet surface, moving the brush slightly to follow the lines of the drawing. Other colors are then applied and allowed to blend into each other transparently so that the pencil sketch remains noticeable. After the painting is completely dry, have students reinforce the idea with black felt marker. Finally, add desired textures.

Evaluation: Based on the ideal combination of color and line as well as the suggestive quality of color in relation to line.

LESSON 22   **Crayon Encaustic Painting**   Advanced

Purpose: To introduce a mode of painting using the wax crayon process.

Materials: Crayons, hot plate, palette knife, brushes, cardboard or masonite.

Procedure: Have students draw on cardboard or masonite. After colors are chosen, crayons are placed in a tin pan or palette set on a hot plate at normal temperature. As crayons melt in the pan, the student should brush or knife the color onto the surface of the masonite or cardboard. This technique is similar to tempera painting, except that the wax crayon dries more quickly. Thus speed in applying the crayon is important. After an area dries, additional color can be applied, resulting in a buildup of color. The color can easily be eradicated by scraping with the palette knife. The design or idea should be properly planned before the process of encaustic painting begins.

Evaluation: Based on the fluidity and clarity of colors as well as on textural qualities.

LESSON 23   **Close-up Tempera Painting**   Intermediate/Advanced

Purpose: To paint in detail a close-up view of a single aspect of nature within its own habitat.

Materials: Tempera paint, brushes, manila paper (18" x 24"), water cups, paint trays, pencils.

Procedure: Have students draw in pencil a single aspect of nature, such as a turtle, frog, fish, bird, spider, or ladybug, enlarged to the size of the paper. Remaining space on the paper should show the creature's natural environment (fish in water, bird in sky). The entire drawing should be painted realistically so as to record all natural detail.

Evaluation: Based on the complexity of detail and technical ability of painting. Background should enhance the entire painting.

Egg in the Nest

LESSON 24   Faraway Tempera Painting   Advanced

Purpose: To paint in detail a single aspect of nature but reverse the size from large to small.

Materials: Tempera paint, brushes, manila paper, water cups, paint trays, pencils.

Procedure: Have the students draw a single aspect of nature about one-tenth the size of the paper. It is important to locate the natural aspect in an appropriate spot in the picture. Since the background space becomes the major part of the painting, the environment must be activated enough to sustain the position of the animal, insect, or object. The drawing should be painted in a detailed, realistic style.

Evaluation: Based on the appropriate location of the single aspect of nature within the natural habitat.

LESSON 25   Word Painting   **Intermediate/Advanced**

Purpose: To incorporate composition, color, and lettering into a single expression.

Materials: Tempera paint, brushes, pencils, white drawing paper, water cups, paint trays.

Procedure: Have students consider various groups of words that form a team, group, or family: nicknames, rock group names, movie stars, athletic teams. Names are then drawn with pencil on large drawing paper in an arrangement of varied sizes and styles. After the composition is complete, it is painted in contrasting colors. Background colors should be subdued (grey, light blue, lavender). Finally, decoration can be added (dots, circles, small words).

Evaluation: Based on the complexity of design, contrast, texture, overall unity, and neatness of execution.

My Friends

LESSON 26   Two Sections of a Single Aspect of Nature   **Advanced**

Purpose: To paint in detail two single aspects of nature, each within its own environment.

Materials: Tempera paint, brushes, water cups, paint trays, white drawing paper, pencils.

Procedure: Have the student divide the paper with pencil into two sections—vertically, horizontally, or diagonally—representing two separate environments, such as sky and land or land and water. Then the student considers and draws an aspect of nature in each area, such as bird in sky, turtle on land. In drawing, neither creature should overlap into the other's environment. Each section of the drawing should survive on its own, but with the use of proper color it should sustain as a single painting. Students paint, texturing areas realistically in detail.

Evaluation: Based on the wholeness of the composition, with details, texture, and blend of color as ingredients, plus careful execution.

LESSON 27   **Three Sections of a Single Aspect of Nature**   Advanced

Purpose: To incorporate three different ideas in three separate sections into a single meaningful painting.

Materials: Tempera paint, brushes, paint trays, water cups, pencils, white drawing paper.

Procedure: Have students divide a large sheet of drawing paper with pencil into three sections representing three natural environments, such as sky, land, and water; water, land, and water; sky separated by two large trees; sky, mountains, and water. Insect or animal life should then be drawn, each within the limits of its environment, but positioned in such a way as to suggest compositional unity. Remember, close-up detail is still important in both the idea and the environment. The drawing should be painted in careful detail.

Evaluation: Based on the unity of the composition and the textural effects of the three environments.

Cityscape

LESSON 28   **Multiplicity of Environments**   **Advanced**

Purpose: To express several aspects of nature, each in its own environment and contributing to the unity of the whole.

Materials: Tempera paint, brushes, water cups, paint trays, pencils, white drawing paper.

Procedure: Have students draw several sections within sections with pencil on large drawing paper, (18" x 24"). For example, if the paper were divided horizontally into sky, water, and land, additional sections would be drawn, such as clouds in the sky and ponds in the land. Each added section should include a natural creature, such as a bird in the cloud as well as in the sky, a duck in the pond as well as a turtle on the land, and a fish in the water. Again, each animal should be positioned to enhance the unity of the whole.

Evaluation: Based on the carefully executed composition of unity and detail.

LESSON 29   **Painting in Cool Colors**   **Beginning/Intermediate/Advanced**

Purpose: To express an emotional mood of a still-life setup.

Materials: Tempera paint, paint trays, water cups, pencils, brushes, white drawing paper.

Procedure: Students should draw an outdoor scene in pencil on large drawing paper. Consideration should be given to the variations of the cool colors of blue, green, and purple. Paint is then applied, lightening and darkening the colors with white and black to create various contrasts. Paint may be applied in a flat or blend pattern.

Evaluation: Based on the "coolness" of the painting and all-over consistency of paint application.

LESSON 30   **Painting in Warm Colors**   **Beginning/Intermediate/Advanced**

Purpose: To create a painting of emotional content, using the warm colors of red, yellow, and orange.

Materials: Tempera paint, water cups, brushes, paint trays, pencils, white drawing paper.

Procedure: Display a still-life setup of a vase of flowers and/or a bowl of fruit. Select flowers and fruit with warm colors. After students have drawn the still life, rely on the visual stimulus for highlights, contrasts, and three-dimensional effects in the painting process. If the drawing is complex, flatly painted areas may sustain the composition more than blended colors.

Evaluation: Based on the emotional content of warmth and the compositional elements of contrast and detail.

LESSON 31   **Painting in Primary Colors**   **Advanced**

Purpose: To execute a painting in the limited use of primary colors.

Materials: Tempera paint, paint trays, water cups, brushes, pencils, white drawing paper.

Procedure: Dictate or set up a stimulus for drawing: landscape, still life, or posed models. Purposely arrange various areas of overlapping planes. Since tinting and shading are prohibited, several small areas should be introduced into the drawing in order to avoid large areas of "empty" colors. After drawing is complete, paint.

   It is very possible that a semi-abstract painting may result. Thus, in order to sustain a unified composition, the colors should be balanced.

Evaluation: Based on the complexity of design and the accurate application of color.

LESSON 32   **Painting in Tones of a Single Primary Color**   **Advanced**

Purpose: To explore within a given activity and medium the possibilities of complete expression with variations of a single color.

Materials: Tempera paint, paint trays, pencils, water cups, brushes, white drawing paper.

Procedure: Students should work from a visual stimulus. It avoids lapses in thinking of ideas for expression. The usual still life is ever-present, so a change of pace may be in order. Set up an all-sports or custodial still life.

   After drawing the stimulus, students should choose one of the three primary colors: red, yellow, or blue. By varying the degree of dark and light added to the color, three-dimensional shapes become evident. The process is continued until the painting is complete.

Evaluation: Based on the range of tints and shades forming a complete and unified painting.

LESSON 33   **Montage and Tempera Painting**   **Intermediate/Advanced**

Purpose: To incorporate the montage expression with tempera paint.

Materials: White drawing paper, magazines, scissors, glue, tempera paint, water cups, paint trays, brushes.

Procedure: After montage is complete, tempera paint is added to empty background spaces. Students may also add paint directly onto the montage material as detail or accent.

Evaluation: Based on the uniform intermixture of paint and montage.

LESSON 34   **Collage and Tempera Painting**   **Intermediate/Advanced**

Purpose: To incorporate the collage expression with tempera paint.

Materials: Collage materials, scissors, glue, white cardboard, tempera paint, brushes, water cups, paint trays, pencils.

Procedure: After collage is complete, have students add tempera paint in spaces unoccupied by collage materials. This may include such sections as sky and water. Students may also paint parts of the collage materials if it suits the idea and enhances the composition.

Evaluation: Based on the unity of collage and tempera paint, and the variety of collage materials in relation to the whole.

The News

LESSON 35   **Finger Painting**   Beginning/Intermediate/Advanced

Purpose: To render flexibly a spontaneous reaction to ideas.

Materials: Finger paint, finger-paint paper, several objects (forks, knives, toothpicks, tooth-brushes, etc.).

Procedure: Have students select colors to fit a particular mood, such as joy, sorrow, hate, or anger. Apply colors to finger-paint paper and "move color" in hand strokes to suit a particular mood, varying the strokes as the hands glide over the paper. After reaching a satisfying design, apply details by scratching into the color with the various tools. This can become a form of sophisticated etching.

Evaluation: Based on the freedom of response to ideas, and the variety of accents and details caused by the various tools.

LESSON 36   **Tempera and Enamel Painting**   **Advanced**

Purpose: To incorporate unique but opposite painting media into a unified composition.

Materials: Tempera paint, colored enamels, brushes, palette knife, paint trays, water cups, drawing paper, masonite or cardboard, gesso, sticks, chalk or charcoal.

Procedure: Have students work from a preliminary sketch, drawing the sketch onto prepared masonite or stiff cardboard with chalk or charcoal. With a stick, drip black enamel onto the drawing, following the contours of the ideas. This drip method will cause suggestive qualities that will later enhance the intuitive appearance. The enamel lines can be broadened with a palette knife to create variations. Other enamel colors are dripped as needed.

After enamel is dry (8 hours), tempera paint colors are applied to the open spaces to correlate with the enamel. The finished product should be a suggestive blend or unity between enamel and tempera paint.

Evaluation: Based on the suggestive quality of the painting as well as the clarity and unity of the paint-enamel combination.

LESSON 37   **Enamel Painting**   **Advanced**

Purpose: To express an idea in a drip-type method hinging on expressionism.

Materials: Colored enamel, prepared masonite, palette knife, brushes, drawing paper, pencils, chalk.

Procedure: Have students first paint a flat enamel color over the entire masonite (2' x 4'), then chalk a drawing onto the masonite. A color is selected and the enamel is dripped over the chalk drawing. Additional colors are dripped over approximately the same area, so that the two colors collide or blend together. A third, fourth, and fifth color repeated in the same fashion will eventually cover most of the masonite. The original color of the masonite will act as a neutral or background color. After the enamels are dry (24 hours), accent areas where needed with a black or white enamel. The entire painting is done by the drip method. The result is an exciting semi-abstract enamel painting, highly suggestive and expressionistic.

Evaluation: Based on the clarity of color and expressionistic appearance. It should be strong in its composition. By the nature of the process, the painting cannot be realistic.

Roots and Trees

LESSON 38   Oil Painting   Intermediate/Advanced

Purpose: To introduce a more permanent medium of expression that allows for fluid blending of color.

Materials: Oil paints, oil brushes, canvas or masonite, palette, palette knife, turpentine, linseed oil, chalk/charcoal, pencils, drawing paper.

Procedure: Have students draw a preliminary sketch in pencil on drawing paper, preferably from a visual stimulus (still life, posed models, landscape) in order to avoid stereotypes. Redraw sketch onto canvas or prepared masonite with charcoal or chalk. Masonite will lend itself to both brush and palette knife.

Since oil paints spread more fluidly than water-base paints, have students consider blending colors, relying upon the colors in the visual stimulus. Students will probaby paint in flat patterns at first, but encourage blending directly on the canvas or masonite. Beware of overblending, causing muddy colors. After painting is completely dry (2 days), accents can be applied with palette knife.

Oil painting demands more than a single attempt. Second and third painting will improve the process.

Evaluation: Based on the fluidity of color and the "feel" of the oil appearance.

Football

LESSON 39   Mixed Media Painting   Advanced

Purpose: To combine several media into a single expression.

Materials: Tempera paint, oil paint, enamels, masonite, chalk, scrap material (cloth, paper), pencils, drawing paper, glue, brushes, palette knife, gesso.

Procedure: Mixed media works best on a hard surface such as masonite. Having drawn with chalk onto the gessoed surface of the masonite, students can attain three-dimensional effects by gluing onto the masonite paper or cloth representing those areas advancing on the picture plane. Oil paints and enamels or water-base paints are then applied in those areas not represented by cloth and/or paper materials.

If desired, paint can be applied over the materials to blend with the other paint. At no time, however, should the applied materials take over the expression.

Evaluation: Based on the blend and compatibility of all media used.

LESSON 40   **Mural Painting**   **Advanced**

Purpose: To give advanced students the experience of enlarging an idea on a vast scale and sharing creative abilities with others.

Materials: An accessible wall, chalk, tempera paints or flat latex, brushes, pencils, drawing paper, fixative.

Procedure: Select a proper setting (classroom wall, cafeteria wall, office, or hallway). Have students prepare a preliminary sketch of proposed ideas. Then redraw on a large scale onto the wall all details of the original sketch. Select medium, preferably water-base paint that can be permanently protected with spray-on fixative. **This project, suited for advanced students, should be thoroughly planned to avoid errors during the painting stage.** Remember, painting on a vertical surface may cause dripping problems. As the painting progresses, encourage blending of color to avoid stiffness.

Other media can be used, such as latex paints, enamels, or oils. Each has its own peculiarities. The choice depends on the abilities of the students.

Evaluation: Based on strength and simplicity. Murals are to be seen from a distance; thus the strength and simplicity of the painting are essential.

CHAPTER III TWO-DIMENSIONAL ACTIVITIES ▬▬

41. Interior Collage
42. Outdoor Collage
43. Abstract Collage
44. Montage of Fantasy
45. Flower Montage
46. Paper Mosaic
47. Tile Mosaic
48. Cereal Mosaic
49. Magazine Mosaic
50. Cutout Silhouettes
51. Color Cutouts
52. Tempera Batik
53. Crayon Batik
54. Stained Glass Window Designs
55. Crayon Resist
56. Cut Tissue-Paper Illustration
57. Torn Tissue-Paper Illustration
58. Black and White Scratchboard
59. Color Scratchboard
60. Linoleum Block Printing (Single-Color)
61. Linoleum Block Printing (Multi-Color)
62. Monoprint
63. Linoleum Block Print with Colored Tissues
64. Glue Line Relief Prints
65. Collographs
66. Woodcut Print
67. Woodcut Relief
68. Fold-over Flower Design
69. Oil Pastel Illustration
70. Oil Pastel Resist
71. Crayon Engraving
72. Multicrayon Engraving
73. Felt-on-Burlap Illustration
74. Interior Design
75. Interior Design with Collage Examples
76. Close-up Painting of Interior Wallpaper
77. Interior Design Collage
78. Placemats
79. Greeting Card Design
80. Pop Drawing Collage
81. Button Mosaic
82. Glass Painting
83. Glass Mosaic
84. Perspective Collage
85. Masking Tape Print
86. String Designs
87. Letter Montage
88. Number Optics
89. Reverse Number Optics
90. Book Jacket Design
91. Record Album Cover Design
92. Miniature Billboard Design
93. Decorative Letter (Inside)
94. Decorative Letter (Outside)
95. Slogan Lettering
96. Advertising Poster
97. The Alphabet
98. Commercial Advertisement
99. Travel Poster
100. Calendar Art Design
101. Stationery Design
102. Window Design for Store Display
103. Protest Poster
104. Menu Design
105. Ink on Wet Paper Illustration
106. Optical Mosaic
107. Crayon Impressionism
108. Contour Drawing on Black Surface
109. Self-Portrait Painting
110. Pen and Ink Perspective

LESSON 41   **Interior Collage**   **Intermediate/Advanced**

Purpose: To incorporate visual and textural contrasts into a single expression.

Materials: White cardboard (12" x 18"), various scrap materials, glue, scissors, pencils.

Procedure: Have students draw on white cardboard the interior of a room, such as kitchen, living room, bedroom, or den, and then furnish it. Materials are selected to glue onto the objects and areas: carpet bits or yarn for floor, wallpaper scraps for walls, bits of wood for furniture. Remind students to contrast both color and texture side by side. Each section and object demands a material, such as paper, cloth, cotton, stones, cereals, or leather. Each material should be cut to fit the prescribed drawing. Balance of color and texture is essential.

Evaluation: Based on compositional unity and attractiveness of room, and variety and originality of materials.

LESSON 42   **Outdoor Collage**   **Intermediate/Advanced**

Purpose: To introduce the sense of touch as well as vision in a single expression.

Materials: White cardboard (12" x 18"), various examples of scrap materials, glue, scissors, pencils.

Procedure: Students draw from memory or visual stimulus an outdoor scene recording such things as buildings, trees, flowers, or fences. Materials are selected to fit within the limits of those objects. If possible, the natural materials—bark, stones, sand, leaves—should be used. Materials are glued in place. Inventive materials may be substituted: cotton for clouds, toothpicks for fences, popsicle sticks for wooden house siding.

Evaluation: Based on the selection of materials and their use in establishing a unified composition.

LESSON 43   **Abstract Collage**   **Beginning/Intermediate/Advanced**

Purpose: To concentrate on textural balance and unity.

Materials: White cardboard, glue, scrap materials, scissors, pencils.

Procedure: Have students record a pencil scribble on white cardboard so that various shapes overlap. Each area should be labelled with the type of textured materials to be used, considering balance and unity. Have students cut these materials and glue them into their proper places. Such materials as cloth, leather, cereals, stones, and buttons are a few examples.

Evaluation: Based on balance and unity of composition and originality and variety of textured materials.

LESSON 44   **Montage of Fantasy**   Intermediate/Advanced

Purpose: To use the compositional elements of magazine advertisements, destroying them and reconstructing them into fantastic compositions.

Materials: White drawing paper, scissors, glue, several magazines.

Procedure: Since this is an improvised approach, have students first cut from magazines several examples of such things as heads, feet, flowers, or cars. The more examples available, the more choices the student has. Have students cut magazine examples carefully and reconstruct them, substituting one object for another: a human leg in place of a dog's tail, a horse's ear replacing a human eye. These elements are glued onto heavy drawing paper. Precise cutting and gluing is essential.

Evaluation: Based on the realistic appearance of fantasy established by precise cutting and pasting, so that one element fits into another naturally.

LESSON 45   **Flower Montage**   Beginning/Intermediate/Advanced

Purpose: To limit the possibility of variation of ideas, but to focus on the variation of a single idea.

Materials: Magazines, white drawing paper, scissors, glue, pencils.

Procedure: Have students cut from magazines colored examples of flowers. Entire flowers and pieces or tracings of alien ideas can be cut and arranged into a colorful flower montage. For the sake of variation, a flower shape can be traced onto a non-flower item such as a soup ad, blue sky, or rugged mountains, then cut out and glued into a flower image. The entire composition is improvised throughout the process of cutting, substituting, arranging, and pasting. Students should eliminate as much negative space as possible by overlapping the flower images.

Evaluation: Based on the excitement generated by the various substitutions and the unity of the whole.

LESSON 46   **Paper Mosaic**   Intermediate/Advanced

Purpose: To cause students to understand and consciously consider part-to-part, part-to-whole, and whole-to-whole relationships. Emphasis is given to how small repetitive units combine to form larger shapes, which then form a unified composition.

Materials: Pencils, newsprint, colored construction paper, white drawing paper, scissors, glue.

Procedure: Have students plan a composition on newsprint, using basic shapes and determining general color scheme. Emphasize the need for bold, simple shapes and strong color contrasts between the shapes. Students then redraw composition on drawing paper, very lightly. Have students select colored construction paper corresponding to the predetermined colors and shapes. Shapes such as squares, rectangles, and triangles are then cut. Paper pieces are pasted onto the background paper, filling in all pencilled shapes with predetermined colors. Background color should show between pieces. Pieces may be cut to fit where necessary. Shapes can be emphasized and interesting rhythms created by following contour of shapes as pieces are laid down. Variety can be achieved by accenting shapes.

Evaluation: Based on effective composition caused by contrasting shapes and colors in addition to the mosaic appearance.

LESSON 47   Tile Mosaic   Intermediate/Advanced

Purpose: To construct a mosaic with small bits of tile to form a complete composition.

Materials: Small bits of colored tiles, glue, masonite or thick white cardboard, pencils, hammer, cloth sack.

Procedure: Have students draw an idea in pencil on white cardboard and select small pieces of ceramic tile to fit contours of the idea. Tile may be broken into smaller bits to fit smaller areas. Students should allow narrow slits of open space between each tile to represent the appearance of a mosaic.

Evaluation: Based on the uniformity and complexity of the composition.

LESSON 48   Cereal Mosaic   Intermediate/Advanced

Purpose: To use common, everyday materials similar to nature and develop a uniform composition.

Materials: Dry cereals (cornflakes, Cheerios, puffed wheat, puffed rice, rice krispies, Wheat Chex, Corn Chex), pencils, white cardboard, glue, fixative (optional).

Procedure: Working from a visual stimulus (still life, posed models, landscape), have students draw in pencil on white cardboard. Various cereals are selected, differing in texture and color. These are arranged and glued to fit the drawing, balancing color and texture. Slits of white cardboard should separate each piece of cereal. The pieces of cereal should be positioned so that a definite pattern emerges. The final product can be sprayed for permanence.

Evaluation: Based on the preciseness of execution and the unity of composition in relation to textures and colors.

LESSON 49 **Magazine Mosaic** Beginning/Intermediate/Advanced

Purpose: To compose a mosaic-like expression relying on newspapers and magazine segments.

Materials: White drawing paper, scissors, glue, pencils, magazines, and newspapers.

Procedure: Have students draw in pencil on white drawing paper an idea relating to the theme of clowns, circuses and/or carnival. Students select pages of colorful ads from magazines and cut them into small squares, triangles, and rectangles. The same is done with newspapers. These pieces are combined in the drawing, allowing narrow slits to separate each piece of applied paper. Remind students to keep a uniform pattern of color within a given area. There should be a proper balance between areas of light (newspaper) and dark (magazine).

Evaluation: Based on the total cohesiveness of the mosaic and the general strength of design.

LESSON 50 **Cutout Silhouettes** Beginning/Intermediate/Advanced

Purpose: To equalize the distribution of positive and negative space (black and white) in a realistic setting.

Materials: White manila paper, black construction paper, pencils, scissors, glue.

Procedure: Have students plan a preliminary sketch on paper using several objects, such as houses, fences, trees, or flowers. Have individual objects redrawn onto black construction paper and cut out. After all objects are cut out of black paper, they are arranged on large white paper so that a silhouette appears. Remind students to be alert to negative space and not to glue in place until the arrangement is complete. White should separate overlapping objects.

Evaluation: Based on the silhouette appearance, balance, and correlation of negative and positive space.

LESSON 51 **Color Cutouts** Beginning/Intermediate/Advanced

Purpose: To manipulate in an improvised manner a selection of colored objects into a total and unified composition.

Materials: Colored construction paper, glue, pencils, scissors, white drawing paper.

Procedure: Have students prepare a preliminary sketch of several objects representing an outdoor scene. The more objects drawn, the less concern for negative space. Have objects redrawn on colored construction paper appropriate to the natural colors of the objects. Objects are cut out and arranged on white drawing paper.

Have several objects cut to allow for versatility. After arrangement of objects is complete, each piece is glued in place. After completion, added details may be cut and glued onto already glued objects.

Evaluation: Based on complexity and balance of composition: color, balance, textured patterns, details, and distribution of positive and negative space.

LESSON 52 **Tempera Batik** **Beginning/Intermediate/Advanced**

Purpose: To introduce students to the unique properties of various media and to demonstrate how they interact with each other. Emphasis is on creating a composition using interactive qualities of various media.

Materials: Tempera paint, white drawing paper, pencils, white chalk, water cups, paint trays, black india ink, sponges, brushes, newspapers.

Procedure: Have students make pencil drawings of subjects associated with bright colors, such as a circus, clowns, flowers, the city at night, or a still life. Encourage close-up drawings to eliminate details that may become lost in the batik process. Have students draw over the pencil lines with chalk, varying line thickness and pressure. Shapes between chalk lines are painted, using bright colors.

When paint is thoroughly dry (overnight), students should place pictures on several layers of newspaper and brush india ink evenly over entire picture surface. Allow ink to dry. Then picture is placed on board and moved about under gently running water. Ink may be washed from painted areas to suit. Caution students to take care. Overwashing will dilute colored areas. Paintings may also be submerged in a water bath to wash ink from painted areas. Sponging and hand wiping can create special effects.

Evaluation: Based on the unique combination of tempera paint and ink in the batik process.

LESSON 53 **Crayon Batik** **Beginning/Intermediate/Advanced**

Purpose: To incorporate crayon illustration with india ink in an effort to sustain a certain type of emotional content by the batik method.

Materials: Crayons, pencils, white drawing paper, black india ink, sponges, brushes.

Procedure: Have students work from themes such as clowns, flowers, or birds, drawing in pencil. Drawings should be simple and large. Crayon is then applied in full intense colors, allowing open lines around each object colored. These open lines should vary in width to create a variety of tensions in the drawing. After completion of coloring, india ink is applied with a wide brush over the entire crayon drawing. Allow to dry. Ink is removed while holding under sink faucet, or sponged gently until enough is removed. The open lines will appear as black accents or outlines. Allow to dry.

Evaluation: Based on the strength of color design in conjunction with the black lines.

LESSON 54   **Stained Glass Window Designs**   **Intermediate/Advanced**

Purpose: To express ideas through a replica-type stained glass window design using transparent colored tissue paper.

Materials: Colored tissue paper, stiff black cardboard, pencils, razor blades or X-acto knives, scissors, scotch tape or masking tape.

Procedure: Have students draw with pencil a preliminary sketch of an idea (religious or civic). The sketch is redrawn on black cardboard, doubling the lines of the drawing to act as braces. Each shape to be cut must be connected with a double line to keep the design intact. The cardboard drawings should be simple, avoiding details. Have students cut the sections inside the double lines with razor blade or X-acto knife. The black cardboard acts as a reinforcement unit, holding the design together as well as separating the colors with a strong contrast.

Laying the colored tissue paper under the specific shape, students trace inside the cut pieces. Then they cut with scissors outside the lines enough so that room is allowed to tape the colored tissue onto the back of the design. This process is continued with each individual piece until the design is complete with color. Finally, the design is carefully taped on a window to display the full beauty of the design.

Evaluation: Based on simplicity and strength of design.

LESSON 55   **Crayon Resist**   **Beginning/Intermediate/Advanced**

Purpose: To express an emotional or atmospheric appearance of an outdoor scene.

Materials: Pencils, white drawing paper, watercolor or tempera paint, paint trays, water cups, brushes, crayons.

Procedure: Have students draw in pencil a scene of the outdoors reflecting a rainy or snowy atmosphere. The drawing is crayoned in, using colors indicative of the atmospheric conditions of the landscape. Watercolor or tempera paint is then brushed over the crayon drawing. Heavily applied crayons will resist the paint more readily than thinly applied crayons.

Evaluation: Based on the atmospheric appearance of the drawing caused by the resist method.

LESSON 56   **Cut Tissue-Paper Illustration**   **Intermediate/Advanced**

Purpose: To present a lead-in to watercolor painting as well as a fluid approach to an idea.

Materials: Colored tissue paper, white drawing paper, glue, scissors, water, brushes, pencils.

Procedure: Have students draw an idea (landscape, flowers, still life, posed models, animals) in pencil on white drawing paper. Colored tissue paper is selected to match the objects drawn. Have geometric tissue-paper shapes cut smaller than the area into which they are to be glued. Glue is prepared diluted with water, brushing first the surface of the paper where the tissue paper is to be applied. The tissue paper is placed into the segment that has been drawn and brushed over to smooth it out. Pieces of tissue paper should overlap as they are glued in place. This overlap causes a textural appearance. This is necessary, especially in large "empty" areas such as sky, water, and land. This process is continued until the illustration is complete. Students should sustain clean edges. Some colors will bleed and cause an undesirable blend. This can be avoided somewhat with less moisture. In some cases, however, it enhances the appearance.

Evaluation: Based on the fluidity of color and the overall composition in addition to transparent effectiveness.

LESSON 57   **Torn Tissue-Paper Illustration**   **Intermediate/Advanced**

Purpose: To exercise a semi-painting approach using colored tissue paper as the medium of expression.

Materials: Colored tissue paper, white drawing paper, pencils, diluted glue, black felt marker.

Procedure: Have students recall an outdoor scene and express it in pencil on white drawing paper. Have them select colored tissue paper and apply to drawing with diluted glue. Have students purposely follow the contours of the preliminary drawing. Colors should overlap to create other colors. The result should be a semi-abstract appearance. Have students follow up with black felt marker lines for accents, decoration, and detail.

Evaluation: Based on the freedom of expression, yet with a certain cohesiveness of overlapping colors.

LESSON 58 Black and White Scratchboard   Intermediate/Advanced

Purpose: To reverse the process of drawing in an etching-like procedure.

Materials: Pencils, black india ink, white crayon, white cardboard, drawing paper, sharp tools, brushes.

Procedure: Have students draw a preliminary sketch on drawing paper. Then have students cover white cardboard heavily with white crayon. Black india ink is applied over the entire surface. Allow to dry. Using a sharp instrument (compass or pointed scissors), students scratch carefully into the blackened surface, referring to preliminary sketches as a guide. This is a spontaneous expression. The student is actually drawing the idea as it is scratched into the black ink.

After line drawings are complete, have students consider textures, details, highlights, and accents. Remember, the reverse is true. Shadows and dark recessive areas remain untouched. Remind students not to overwork.

Evaluation: Based on the sharpness of detail and clarity of expression. Emotional content, the appearance of a mood, should be evident.

LESSON 59 Color Scratchboard   Beginning/Intermediate/Advanced

Purpose: To create an expression of emotional content using the reverse process of drawing.

Materials: Pencils, crayons, white cardboard, drawing paper, black india ink, sharp tools, brushes.

Procedure: Have students color heavily onto white cardboard several areas of different colors in an abstract fashion, locating them on the white cardboard according to a preliminary sketch. Have colored cardboard covered completely with black india ink, and allow to dry.

Using a sharp tool, students scratch into the surface, referring to the preliminary sketch as a guide. Colors on the cardboard should correspond to objects in the preliminary drawing. Remember, this is a searching activity. The objects of the preliminary drawing are hidden under the colored crayons and ink. So remind students to proceed slowly. Again, accent, texture, and detail should be added where needed.

Evaluation: Based on the use of black as a contrast and accent to color, and on the strength of composition and color unity.

LESSON 60   Linoleum Block Printing (Single-Color)   Beginning/Intermediate/Advanced

Purpose: To introduce the printing process.

Materials: Linoleum block, linoleum tools, pencils, drawing paper, razor blades, carbon paper, printer's ink, brayer, printing paper.

Procedure: Have students sketch on drawing paper an idea the same size as the cut linoleum. Sketch is placed over carbon paper and both are placed on the linoleum and traced with pointed pencil. Sketch is removed from linoleum and the cutting process is begun with a V-shaped cutter or razor blade. Tell students not to cut too deeply at first. They should continue working with the cutter and other tools until all lines and textures are cut. Then they roll ink over the cut and print. More cutting may be necessary after viewing the first print. Have students experiment with different colored inks as well as colored paper.

Evaluation: Based on the clarity of print and the mood or complexity of design.

LESSON 61   Linoleum Block Printing (Multi-Color)   Intermediate/Advanced

Purpose: To expand the possibilities of the print process.

Materials: Linoleum block, linoleum tools, pencils, drawing paper, razor blades, carbon paper, printer's inks, brayer, colored printing paper.

Procedure: Have students design and cut the linoleum as usual, but cut lightly to start. Have students make several prints, each on different colored paper. Next, the linoleum block should be cleaned and more of the design cut away. Then it is inked again, but with a different color. This will print on top of the first print. The color of the first print will now show where the area was just cut. If more color or detail is wanted, cutting, inking, and printing can continue in the same way.

Evaluation: Based on the clarity of design and the number of colors used effectively.

LESSON 62   **Monoprint**   **Beginning/Intermediate/Advanced**

Purpose: To experience the print process in a simple and expressive manner.

Materials: Inking plate, printing ink, roller, printing paper, slightly pointed instrument, piece of glass or prepared masonite.

Procedure: Have students roll printing ink onto a piece of glass or prepared masonite and even out the ink. A sheet of printing paper is laid lightly onto the inked surface. The paper is held in a stationary position as a drawing is made on the paper. The degree of pressure applied to the paper determines the tone darkness or lightness. Remind students to be careful that finger marks don't become a part of the design! After drawing is complete, the drawing paper is removed. The final product is the reverse of the original drawing.

Evaluation: Based on the various tones of light and dark and the instinctive quality of the drawing.

LESSON 63   **Linoleum Block Print with Colored Tissues**   **Beginning/Intermediate/Advanced**

Purpose: To incorporate the block print with additional media. To correlate a black line cut with shapes of color.

Materials: Colored tissue paper, glue, scissors, pencils, heavy white printing paper, linoleum block, linoleum cutters, printing ink, printing plate, roller.

Procedure: Have students cut a linoleum print as usual. However, instead of printing onto a single white sheet of paper, have students prepare the paper beforehand with free-form pieces of colored tissue paper. Have tissue papers cut or torn and glued in appropriate locations on the printing paper. After the colored tissues are securely glued, the black-inked cut linoleum is positioned over it and pressed heavily onto the paper. Then the ink block is removed. The result, a colorfully contrasted linoleum block print.

Evaluation: Based on the unified relationship between the black line cut and the colored tissue background.

LESSON 64   **Glue Line Relief Prints**   **Beginning/Intermediate/Advanced**

Purpose: To use a simple print method for imaginative results.

Materials: Masonite/printing plate, printing ink, glue, roller, printing paper, pencils, drawing paper, stiff white cardboard, Elmer's glue, tissue paper.

38

Procedure: Have students draw with pencil a preliminary sketch of a visual stimulus (still life, flowers, posed models), then redraw sketch onto stiff white cardboard. Carefully drip Elmer's glue onto the pencil sketch, narrowing or widening lines as the glue flows out of the squeeze bottle. After the glue is completely dry (2 hours), roll ink over the design. When ink has been consistently applied, place tissue paper or newsprint over the design and roll or rub gently with fingers or palm of hand. Peel the paper off the plate. The print will be more consistent if the background is also rubbed.

Evaluation: Based on the unity of the line and space of the background.

LESSON 65 Collographs   Beginning/Intermediate/Advanced

Purpose: To introduce a simple but exciting method of printmaking.

Materials: Masonite or heavy cardboard, glue, scissors, ink brayer, water-base printing ink, newsprint or tissue paper, shellac, utility brush.

Procedure: Have students cut flowers, animals, people, or other ideas into various shapes and sizes to be glued onto masonite or cardboard in a unified composition. After ideas are glued securely (a coat of shellac helps prevent peeling), roll ink over the plate carefully and evenly. Place newsprint or tissue paper over plate and press carefully, rubbing with the hands and fingers. Remove the paper quickly so that the print does not stick to the plate.

Evaluation: Based on the complexity and unification of the design as well as the emotional content.

LESSON 66 Woodcut Print   Advanced

Purpose: To incorporate a wood grain with a woodcut in the process of printmaking.

Materials: Wood block (pine, cherry, maple), printing ink, printing paper, ink brayer, ink palette, woodcutting tools, pencils, carbon paper, drawing paper.

Procedure: The woodcut is similar to the linoleum cut except for consideration given to the wood grain. Have students execute a preliminary sketch on drawing paper. Redraw or transfer with carbon paper onto the wood block, drawing with the grain wherever possible. This will diminish the probability of wood chipping. White pine works well for this. Sometimes the student may wish to cause chipping to suit the idea.

Cut into the wood with cutting tools where the lines are drawn. After the line cut is complete, make a print. This initial print enables one to see where textured and/or full areas should be cut. Do several prints until a satisfactory one is made.

Evaluation: Based on the unification of the cut and the grain of the wood.

LESSON 67 **Woodcut Relief** **Advanced**

Purpose: To use the woodcut as an art form in and of itself.

Materials: Wood block, printing ink, printing paper, ink brayer, ink palette, woodcutting tools, fixative (optional).

Procedure: After several prints are made, have students wash the wood block thoroughly. Additional cuts are made if desirable. The block can be displayed as the cut appears, or colored ink may be applied, allowed to dry, and sprayed with fixative. If "oil-based inks" are used, no spray is necessary.

Evaluation: Based on the final appearance of the wood block as a wood relief.

LESSON 68 **Fold-over Flower Design** **Beginning/Intermediate/Advanced**

Purpose: To formulate a complex painting from a spontaneous form of experimentation.

Materials: White drawing paper, tempera paints, brushes, water cups, paint trays, black felt markers.

Procedure: Have students apply brushloads of tempera paint in different colors onto the right side of white drawing paper, adhering to a mental image of flowers. Paper is then folded in half so that the left side covers the right side. Rub or press gently. Unfold the paper. The same design will appear on both sides of the paper. Using this as a beginning, additional flowers are painted to form a full flower painting. Allow to dry. Black felt marker may accent or contrast the flower forms. Details may also be considered.

Evaluation: Based on the complexity and unity of the composition.

LESSON 69 **Oil Pastel Illustration** **Beginning/Intermediate/Advanced**

Purpose: To introduce a method of blending color into a unified composition.

Materials: Oil pastels, white drawing paper, pencils, colored construction paper, erasers, paper towels, colored chalk.

Procedure: Have students work from a visual stimulus (landscape, still life, posed models) in order to comprehend fully the mixture and blend of color as well as the elimination of an overabundance of negative space. Have the drawing penciled on large white drawing paper (18" x 24"). Add details. Using the oil pastels, have students blend and contrast colors as they appear in the visual stimulus. Rubbing with erasers or paper toweling will make the blending easier. If colored papers are used as the drawing surface, then colored chalk should be used to draw the idea.

40

Evaluation: Based on the brilliance of color and the complexity of color blends and contrasts into a unified composition.

Trees

LESSON 70   Oil Pastel Resist   Beginning/Intermediate/Advanced

Purpose: This exercise provides a more colorful and detailed follow-up to the crayon resist (Lesson 55) since these color blends are more easily attainable.

Materials: Oil pastels, white or colored drawing paper, pencils, tempera paint, brushes, paint trays, water cups.

Procedure: This is a method similar to oil pastel illustration except for the allowance of space between each of the drawn objects. Again, have students choose a theme representing bright colors such as clowns, flowers, or birds. Have the theme drawn on white or light pastel drawing paper. Proceed with the oil pastels as usual, but allow empty spaces between each object. Students then apply black tempera over the entire drawing, the black paint filling in those areas that were left untouched. The more solid the pressure placed on the oil pastels, the more resistance given the tempera paint.

Evaluation: Based on the use of the black tempera paint both in the resist process and the untouched areas.

LESSON 71   **Crayon Engraving**   **Beginning/Intermediate/Advanced**

Purpose: To use mixed media to express a uniform composition.

Materials: Crayons, black poster paint, white drawing paper, pencils, brushes, paint trays, water cups, white cardboard, sharp etching instruments, newsprint (optional).

Procedure: If the idea is to be a mental image, have students draw it first on newsprint for the sake of organization. Once completed, the drawing is transferred onto white cardboard. If working from a visual image such as still life or landscape, the idea may be drawn directly onto the white cardboard. The student should then proceed to color in crayon all areas of the completed drawing, following up with an application of black tempera. Allow to dry. Then have students draw with a variety of etching tools, guessing at the design underneath or referring to the visual stimulus. If the design is a mental image, refer to the original drawing on newsprint. This allows instinctive responses that may alter the course of the initial idea.

Evaluation: Based on the emotional content and the proper distribution of black tempera paint, in addition to composition and textured details.

LESSON 72   **Multicrayon Engraving**   **Beginning/Intermediate/Advanced**

Purpose: To introduce a crayon-over-crayon technique of etching.

Materials: Crayons, white poster board, pencils, sharp instruments such as sloyd knives, compasses, pins, pointed scissors.

Procedure: Have students first draw an idea onto white poster board with a slick finish. Then have the entire drawing colored, first with light colors such as yellow, orange, light green, light blue, or lavender. Next, crayon each color a second time with a different color, then a third and a fourth. Finally, coat the entire drawing with black crayon.

Using sharp tools, have students scratch or etch lines through the crayon layers, piercing the top layer only in some cases and the bottom in others. The variation of color tiers incised will cause a variety of color nuances. Allow the overlay of black crayon to remain where desired. Details and textures are important.

Evaluation: Based on the dramatic impact of the use of black in contrast to the brilliant colors.

LESSON 73 **Felt-on-Burlap Illustration** Intermediate/Advanced

Purpose: To introduce fabric materials into a unified composition.

Materials: Colored felt, burlap, scissors, glue, pencils, white drawing paper.

Procedure: Have students draw a preliminary design or illustration on newsprint to the exact scale to be used on the burlap. Select felt colors to be used and the color of the burlap for the background. Have students cut out the objects drawn on the newsprint and trace onto the colored felt. Cut from the colored felt and arrange onto the colored burlap, following the preliminary sketch as much as possible. When all pieces of colored felt are arranged, glue down securely. The finished illustration can be used as a wall hanging, a piece of upholstery, or a framed "masterpiece."

Evaluation: Based on the compositional unity, the variety of shapes, sizes, and colors of the felt; the compatibility of positive and negative space; textural qualities; and emotional content.

LESSON 74 **Interior Design** Intermediate/Advanced

Purpose: To introduce an interior design project.

Materials: Tempera/watercolor paint, paint trays, water cups, brushes, heavy white drawing paper, pencils.

Procedure: Have students draw in perspective the interior of a room (kitchen, living room, bedroom). Add drawings of wall furnishings, drapes, carpeting, and furniture. Render in watercolor or tempera paint a color scheme appropriate to the room. Have students paint textural qualities of furniture, interior walls, and floor. Finally, accents and details may be added.

Evaluation: Based on the completeness, unity, and appropriateness of interior to type of room.

LESSON 75 **Interior Design with Collage Examples** Intermediate/Advanced

Purpose: To incorporate textural examples into interior design.

Materials: Scrap materials, pencils, heavy white drawing paper, fine-line black felt markers, glue, scissors, razor blades or X-acto knives.

Procedure: Have students make a second drawing in pencil on heavy white drawing paper or white cardboard, including furniture and furnishings. Instead of painting, have the entire drawing outlined in fine-line black felt marker. Allow room on the white paper for a series of three-inch squares to be drawn adjacent to the interior design of the room. Select, cut, and glue onto these squares examples of such things as carpeting, tile, and wallpaper to be used in the interior design.

Evaluation: Based on the selection and compatibility of examples and their compositional unity with the design as a whole.

LESSON 76   Close-up Painting of Interior Wallpaper   Advanced

Purpose: To introduce allover patterns as examples of wallpaper design in detail.

Materials: Tempera paint, paint trays, water cups, brushes, large sheets of white drawing paper, wallpaper samples, pencils.

Procedure A: Cut individual motifs from samples of small-patterned wallpaper. Have students choose one motif apiece, then have them enlarge their designs to easily workable size (at least twice the original size). In pencil, students will repeat the motif at regular intervals, covering the paper from edge to edge. Then have students carefully paint their "wallpaper," duplicating the colors of the original motif.

Evaluation: Based on the neatness and accuracy of the design.

Procedure B: After students have completed exercise A, have them each design an original motif, using geometric shapes, natural forms, or other stimuli. Have them then repeat this motif as above, covering the entire sheet of paper. Carefully planning their colors, students will then paint their "wallpaper," making sure that each motif is a replica of the first.

Evaluation: Based on the appropriateness of the design and the neatness and accuracy of the execution.

LESSON 77   Interior Design Collage   Advanced

Purpose: To incorporate color, line, and textural qualities into an attractive room interior.

Materials: Pencils, heavy white drawing paper or white cardboard, tempera paint, paint trays, brushes, water cups, collage materials, glue, X-acto knives or razor blades.

Procedure: Have students redraw room interior in pencil on heavy white drawing paper. Then have all areas of the room painted that are not to be covered with collage materials. Carefully cut with scissors or X-acto knives materials for such things as carpeting, wallpaper, and paneling, and glue in place onto the design.

   The final result should display an attractive room interior, indicating the color scheme and textural accessories.

Evaluation: Based on the compatibility of color and texture, and the overall attractiveness and appropriateness of the room interior.

LESSON 78   Placemats   Beginning/Intermediate/Advanced

Purpose: To design placemats for seasonal occasions.

Materials: Pencils, white drawing paper, colored construction paper, tempera paint, paint trays, brushes, water cups, clear varnish.

Procedure: This activity should be introduced to meet a particular seasonal need (Christmas, Easter, Mother's Day). Have students draw a seasonal symbol three inches square to each corner of colored construction paper of their choice. Diminish the size of the symbol and repeat along each edge of the construction paper as a border design. After drawing is complete, apply tempera paint in typical seasonal colors. Finally, coat entire placemat with a thin layer of clear varnish for permanency.

Evaluation: Based on choice of symbols and colors appropriate to the occasion.

LESSON 79   Greeting Card Design   Beginning/Intermediate/Advanced

Purpose: To create greeting cards for seasonal occasions by the stenciling method.

Materials: Heavy tagboard, cardboard, pencils, scissors, X-acto knives/razor blades, appropriate greeting card paper, stencil brushes, tempera paint, paint trays, brushes, water cups.

Procedure: Have students draw onto heavy tagboard or cardboard a seasonal symbol. Cut entire symbol out with scissors. Inner shapes of the design can be cut with X-acto knives or single-edge razor blades. Cut several designs to insure clean, accurate application of paint. Select, cut, and fold appropriate paper to suit the size and shape desired. Place design symbol onto selected paper, and using stencil brush, apply paint onto the open spaces of the design. The design can be applied on the inside or the outside of the card, or both. Allow space for seasonal message inside the card. Repeat the process to meet your seasonal needs.

Evaluation: Based on the clean appearance, choice of colors, and general layout of the composition.

LESSON 80   Pop Drawing Collage   Beginning/Intermediate/Advanced

Purpose: To incorporate the pop drawing technique with collage materials.

Materials: Colored drawing pencils, white drawing paper, gum and/or candy wrappers, scissors, glue.

Procedure: Have students collect several candy and gum wrappers. Copy, but enlarge each wrapper, displaying dark and light contrast, details, and overlapping. Students should allow space within the drawing so that the original wrappers can be glued in place. After pencil drawing is complete, cut wrappers in parts and glue at angles opposite to those drawn. Wrappers should be glued to appear as if they go underneath those drawn. Since the colors of the wrappers will appear much stronger than those executed in pencil, thought must be given to the size and shape of the original wrappers.

After all wrappers are glued in place, strengthen those already drawn to meet the strength of the colors on the wrappers.

Evaluation: Based on the total unity of composition and balance of color and black-and-white tones.

LESSON 81   Button Mosaic   Beginning/Intermediate/Advanced

Purpose: To execute a mosaic design with a single common material.

Materials: Variety of buttons, glue, masonite or heavy white cardboard, pencils, newsprint, carbon paper.

Procedure: Have students draw in pencil on newsprint a preliminary sketch of an idea, such as flowers, animals, or fruit bowls. Trace the design through carbon paper onto the masonite or cardboard. Select buttons according to size, shape, and color to fit into designed drawing. Glue securely. Be alert to contrast and texture relationships.

Evaluation: Based on the various combinations of color, size, and textures as a total composition.

LESSON 82   Glass Painting   Intermediate/Advanced

Purpose: To use the painting medium as a stained glass project.

Materials: Pane of plate glass or plastic (size appropriate to use), white cardboard, fine-line black felt markers, oil or tempera paint, brushes, masking tape, two-way tape, etching tools, compass point or X-acto knife.

Procedure: Have students design on white cardboard an idea for a stained-glass window. Cut each part of the drawing out and arrange onto glass. Trace around the edge of each part of the cut design separately with fine-line black felt marker until all parts of the whole are evident on the glass. Have all sections painted with varied colors, leaving open a narrow slit or line between each color. Allow to dry. Then have students paint the open lines in black in widths between ¼" and ½". Allow to dry.

Using two-way tape, cut 4 pieces into ½″ squares and place on each corner of the reverse side of the glass. Place glass against window and press down. Reinforce glass with additional tape if desired.

Evaluation: Based on appearance of the stained glass design and the strength and clarity of color.

LESSON 83   Glass Mosaic   **Intermediate/Advanced**

Purpose: To use a common commodity in an artistic expression.

Materials: Colored glass bottles or pieces of colored glass, hammer, burlap sack, glue, masonite or wood, pencils, newsprint, carbon paper.

Procedure: Have students draw a flower design on newsprint and transfer it through carbon paper onto painted wood or masonite. Colored glass bottles should be placed in heavy burlap sacks, tied, and placed on a cement surface. Using a hammer or mallet, crush glass into small bits. Arrange the bits of glass on the painted masonite design, and glue them. Color contrast and balance are important.

Evaluation: Based on unified composition and variety of color arrangement.

LESSON 84   Perspective Collage   **Beginning/Intermediate/Advanced**

Purpose: To correlate perspective drawing with recession and advancement of textural details.

Materials: White cardboard or posterboard, glue, scissors, X-acto knives, pencils, scrap materials, newsprint.

Procedure: Have students draw a preliminary sketch on newsprint of a one- or two-point perspective. Note the types of materials to be used for the collage (corrugated cardboard, panelling, wallpaper textures, carpeting, for instance). Complete the drawing in pencil. Redraw onto white poster board. Glue materials with detailed textures and bright colors near the forefront of the drawing to make buildings, etc., recede in space. Glue less detailed, less bright materials further back in the picture plane. The effect should be one of recession and advancement caused by color, detail, and texture of the glued-on materials. Add close-up details like window frames, if desired.

Evaluation: Based on the perspective effects of the collage materials and unified composition.

LESSON 85   **Masking Tape Print**   **Beginning/Intermediate/Advanced**

Purpose: To execute a print using a simple method.

Materials: Pencils, drawing paper, masking tape, printing ink, ink brayer, printing paper, ink plate, heavy cardboard or tagboard, newsprint (optional).

Procedure: Have students work from visual stimulus, such as a flower still life, and draw preliminary sketch on newsprint. Redraw on cardboard. Apply masking tape cut to fit the lines of the drawing. Build up taped areas with second and third layers, just short of a relief. Remember, the untaped areas will print white, so enough tape should be applied to avoid open spaces. Roll ink over the design and print on newsprint. Repeat process several times.

Evaluation: Based on the clarity or suggestive quality of the print.

LESSON 86   **String Designs**   **Beginning/Intermediate/Advanced**

Purpose: To motivate students to use a simple approach to doodling and develop it into a highly imaginative expression.

Materials: String, large white drawing paper, tempera paint, paint trays, fine-line black felt markers.

Procedure: Have students fold large white drawing paper in half. They then dip a piece of string into a single color of tempera paint and lay it on the inside of the paper. After folding back the paper, press and rub gently. Pull the string out while paper is still folded, or unfold the paper and remove the string. Repeat process with several colors, placing each string in a different position to cause an abstract design.
    After several colors have been used, allow to dry. The design will be an all-over pattern covering the entire paper. After serious study of the design, apply felt marker to enhance the design, either in an abstract fashion or by developing a world of fantasy.

Evaluation: Based on the total development of the initial design into an advanced composition.

LESSON 87   **Letter Montage**   **Beginning/Intermediate/Advanced**

Purpose: To incorporate a variety of letters into a montage composition.

Materials: Magazines, newspapers, glue, scissors, large white drawing paper.

48

Procedure: Have students select various styles, sizes, and colors of letters and words from magazines and newspapers. Cut and arrange onto large white drawing paper. Try several arrangements before finally gluing in place. Look for balance of color and styles.

Evaluation: Based on variety of sizes, shapes, styles, and colors of letters and total unification.

LESSON 88   Number Optics   **Intermediate/Advanced**

Purpose: To exploit recession and advancement of letters on a neutral background.

Materials: White drawing paper, tempera paint, paint trays, water cups, brushes.

Procedure: Have students paint entire white drawing paper with nuances of grey tones, in areas ranging in size from 3 to 6 square inches, blending the tones as they are painted. Allow to dry. With pencil, draw several variations of different sized numbers over the grey background.

    Have numbers painted one by one in colors ranging from dark red to bright red to white, considering at all times the effect of the number color on the grey background. A white number will advance on the grey background and a dark red one will recede. Continue loading the background with numbers until filled to capacity.

Evaluation: Based on the effectiveness of receding and advancing colors.

LESSON 89   Reverse Number Optics   **Intermediate/Advanced**

Purpose: To exploit effects of a bright background on the muted colors of numbers.

Materials: White drawing paper, tempera paint, paint trays, water cups, brushes, pencils.

Procedure: Have students paint entire white paper with a bright red color. Allow to dry. Draw several numbers of various sizes on the red background in pencil. Paint numbers ranging in color from white to black, considering placement. Squeeze in as many numbers as possible.

Evaluation: Based on the effectiveness of red background in relation to muted numbers.

LESSON 90   Book Jacket Design   **Beginning/Intermediate/Advanced**

Purpose: To design a book jacket cover using lettering and illustration.

Materials: White drawing paper, pencils, tempera paint, paint trays, water cups, brushes.

Procedure: Have students select or invent a book title. Make a preliminary sketch of layout, including title, author, and illustration relevant to story. Try an unusual arrangement. After the drawing is complete, redraw on 9" x 12" white drawing paper. Consider any changes first. Select colors to suit title, and paint letters and illustration. Allow negative space to work as part of design.

Evaluation: Based on the compatibility and unified relationship between title, author's name, and illustration. Style and color of lettering is important.

LESSON 91   Record Album Cover Design   Beginning/Intermediate/Advanced

Purpose: To design a circular record-album cover using lettering, color, and illustration.

Materials: White cardboard or poster board, tempera paint, brushes, paint trays, water cups, pencils, compass, newsprint.

Procedure: Have students draw a 12" circle on newsprint. Lay in lettering and illustration interpreting a popular rock, country, or blues group. make color notations. After completion of sketch, have students redraw design onto white poster board. Apply tempera paint following the color notes of the preliminary sketch. Try an unusual contemporary composition.

Evaluation: Based on the unique compatibility of lettering style, color, and illustration.

LESSON 92   Miniature Billboard Design   Beginning/Intermediate/Advanced

Purpose: To explore the ingredients of billboard design.

Materials: Newsprint, pencils, white drawing paper, tempera paint, paint trays, water cups, brushes.

Procedure: Have students draw a preliminary sketch for a billboard in pencil on newsprint, considering the name of the establishment, type of services rendered, hours of service, distance to the establishment, and directions for arrival. After this preliminary drawing is complete, redraw it on white drawing paper. Paint appropriate areas of design, realizing the distance from which the billboard will be viewed.

Evaluation: Based on the attractiveness of design and the simplicity of the message.

LESSON 93   Decorative Letter (Inside)   Beginning/Intermediate/Advanced

Purpose: To decorate within a given letter shape while sustaining the letter's identification.

Materials: Newsprint, pencils, white drawing paper, tempera paint, paint trays, water cups, brushes.

Procedure: Have students do preliminary sketch first on newsprint. Each student should consider all letters of the alphabet and choose the one that best suits the individual. Have students redraw the letter on white drawing paper (9″ x 12″). Then have the design decorated within the letter with objects that relate to the style or type of letter. Such things as flowers, geometric shapes, and smaller repeat letters can be considered. Once the letter is completely designed, tempera paint should be applied.

Evaluation: Based on the appropriate application of color to the design itself.

LESSON 94   Decorative Letter (Outside)   Beginning/Intermediate/Advanced

Purpose: To decorate outside a given letter shape while sustaining the letter's identification.

Materials: Newsprint, pencils, white drawing paper, tempera paint, paint trays, brushes, water cups.

Procedure: Have students do preliminary sketch first on newsprint. They should consider all letters of the alphabet and choose the one that best fits a descriptive picture or story. Discourage students from changing letters into objects. The letter must sustain itself regardless of the amount of decoration provided. Have students redraw the design onto white drawing paper. Apply tempera paint using color appropriate to the design.

Evaluation: Based on the strength of the letter regardless of the amount of decoration.

LESSON 95   Slogan Lettering   Intermediate/Advanced

Purpose: To encourage proper lettering in a disciplined and professional manner.

Materials: White or colored poster board (10″ x 18″), pencils, rulers, fine-line and blunt black felt markers, newsprint.

Procedure: Have students select a famous or popular slogan or verse. They should practice letters and spacing on newsprint. Simple block letters are preferred at first. After sufficient practice, have students lay out the slogan or poem on the precut white poster board. Outline all letters of the slogan with a fine-line black felt marker. Then fill in letters with a blunt-nosed black marker. Allow enough space at the ends of the poster board so that letters are not crowded or hyphenated.

Evaluation: Based on neatness and professional appearance.

LESSON 96   **Advertising Poster**   Beginning/Intermediate/Advanced

Purpose: To advertise a salable product in the form of a poster.

Materials: Newsprint, pencils, white poster board, black felt markers, rulers, tempera paint, paint trays, water cups, brushes.

Procedure: Have students select a commercial product to be advertised in a market of their choice. Have it designed first on newsprint, including the name of the product and an illustration of it, as well as its description. Consider overlapping for compositional unity. After completion of the preliminary sketch, have students redraw the design on white poster board. Make sure that the style of lettering is appropriate to the object being advertised. After design is complete on poster board, have tempera paint applied. Black felt markers can be used for accents, details, and/or strengthening letters.

Evaluation: Based on the professional appearance of poster in relation to lettering, color, balance, and composition.

LESSON 97   **The Alphabet**   Beginning/Intermediate/Advanced

Purpose: To practice styles of lettering and spacing.

Materials: Newsprint, pencils, white poster board, rulers, black felt markers.

Procedure: Have students draw each letter of the alphabet on newsprint, considering spacing of each letter. After mastery of each letter, have students redraw the entire alphabet on white poster board. Ink in with black felt marker, ruling the outside of each letter. Finally, proceed to fill in each letter with blunt-nosed markers.

Evaluation: Based on the uniformity of letters and the proper spacing of each.

LESSON 98   **Commercial Advertisement**   Beginning/Intermediate/Advanced

Purpose: To make an attractive advertising layout of a commercial product.

Materials: Newsprint, pencils, white poster board, tempera paint, paint trays, water cups, brushes, fine-line black felt markers, rulers.

Procedure: Remind students that this is not a poster, but a commercial layout for a magazine ad, complete with copy. Have students design a commercial product, including name, description, and illustration of the product, together with copy to describe the product more fully. After first designing on newsprint, have students redraw onto white poster board or white drawing paper. Apply tempera paint where needed (major letters, illustration). Fine-line black felt marker should be used for copy lettering.

Evaluation: Based on neatness, simplicity, unified composition, color accents, readability, and general professional appearance.

LESSON 99 Travel Poster   Beginning/Intermediate/Advanced

Purpose: To make an attractive poster by means of color, lettering, and composition of a scene or place worth visiting.

Materials: Newsprint, pencils, white or colored poster board, tempera paint, paint trays, brushes, water cups, rulers, black felt markers.

Procedure: Have students select a site, city, town, state, or country, or invent a "paradise." Have the design first sketched out on newsprint, with illustration and lettering. Suggest unusual composition with the focal point off-center, and encourage overlapping. Students could try optical, abstract, or surrealistic designs. After designs are completely drawn, transfer or redraw onto poster board. Apply tempera paint and felt marker for effects. Try unusual color schemes.

Evaluation: Based on neatness, accuracy of lettering, and general attractive appearance.

LESSON 100 Calendar Art Design   Intermediate/Advanced

Purpose: To incorporate numbers, letters, and illustration into a practical composition.

Materials: Newsprint, pencils, white poster board, rulers, tempera paint, brushes, paint trays, water cups, black felt markers.

Procedure: Have students select a shape and size for calendar design (tall and vertical, square, or short and horizontal). Present layout first on newsprint. Have students choose their favorite month as a guide to the entire year's portrayal. The design should incorporate letters, numbers, illustration, and color. The type of lettering should be consistent throughout the calendar, with each month devoted to a single theme. Attention should also be given to holidays. The illustration should be attractive enough to display as a wall hanging or a table or desk object. Yet it should be practical. Once the designs are acceptable, have students redraw them on white poster board. Apply tempera paint to the illustrations. The black felt marker should be used for both letters and numbers.

Evaluation: Based on practicality and aesthetic content in relation to the use of compositional ingredients such as color, contrast, and appropriate use of letters and numbers.

LESSON 101   **Stationery Design**   Beginning/Intermediate/Advanced

Purpose: To design a stationery note card and envelope incorporating lettering and decoration.

Materials: White or colored drawing paper, tempera paint, paint trays, water cups, brushes, pencils, newsprint, rulers, fine-line black felt markers.

Procedure: Have each student do a preliminary drawing on the newsprint of his or her name and address. Have the student's favorite symbol drawn in the upper left- and lower right-hand corners. Center and print name and address on top of the paper. Repeat the name and address on the upper left-hand corner of the envelope. Have the symbol redrawn on fine quality white or colored paper from the preliminary sketch. Apply tempera paint on symbols and execute lettering in fine-line black felt markers, on both paper and envelope. Remind students that this is a design.

Evaluation: Based on the attractive quality of the symbol and general layout of both card and envelope.

LESSON 102   **Window Design for Store Display**   Intermediate/Advanced

Purpose: To design and execute layout for a store window display.

Materials: White drawing paper, tempera paint, pencils, paint trays, watercolor paint, water cups, brushes, rulers, felt markers, newsprint.

Procedure: Have students select a type of merchandise window to design, such as jewelry, shoes, clothing, candy, magazine, or books. Shape and size of window are important. Once type, shape, and size have been chosen, students should plan season of display. Proceed to draw the layout on newsprint, complete with color and lettering. Once complete, redraw onto white drawing paper. Apply tempera paint or watercolor where needed. Felt markers may be used for accents and details.

Evaluation: Based on unusual window shape and convincing salesmanship. Follow-up for independent study would be actual dressing of the window within the school, and eventually in the community.

LESSON 103   **Protest Poster**   Beginning/Intermediate/Advanced

Purpose: To execute a strong, simple poster with a direct message.

Materials: Poster board, felt markers, tempera paint, paint trays, water cups, newsprint, pencils, brushes.

Procedure: Have students sketch on newsprint a message, in words, to be used. Only important words should be considered. Also to be considered is the distance from which signs are to be viewed. After preliminary layout, transfer to poster board or tagboard. Have students paint with broad strokes of dark or bright colors, keeping letters simple in structure.

Evaluation: Based on suitability of the poster to the purpose involved, and on simplicity and strength of design.

LESSON 104   Menu Design   Beginning/Intermediate/Advanced

Purpose: To design an attractive cover for a restaurant/lounge menu.

Materials: Newsprint, pencils, white or colored paper, tempera paint, paint trays, water cups, brushes.

Procedure: Have students draw preliminary sketch on newsprint of layout for menu cover. Gear it to the style and taste of a particular clientele, such as the rich, the elderly, workers, sports fans, business people. Have students design a symbol (such as a crest) or an initial to be used as a focal point. Also include the name of the establishment, with lettering representative of the clientele. Fancy or plain border designs could also be considered.

Evaluation: Based on simplicity, readability, and appropriateness to clientele.

LESSON 105   Ink on Wet Paper Illustration   Intermediate/Advanced

Purpose: To use ink on wet paper, controlling the ink's "accidental" flow.

Materials: Black india ink, ink pens, brushes, white drawing paper, water cups, sponges, newsprint, pencils.

Procedure: Have students sketch several ideas on newsprint with pencil. Have one of the sketches redrawn onto large white drawing paper. Wet the paper with sponge or brush. While the paper remains wet, drop ink from a pen onto the wet surface, allowing ink to follow the pencil sketch. Try to control the flow of ink so that puddles of water are avoided. The ink will spread profusely where water sets on the paper, and less where the surface of the paper is less wet. Eventually, control of the ink, water, and pen will become easier. Try to block out as much of the white paper as possible. When complete, let dry. Apply dry ink lines over the drawing for accents, textures, and details.

Evaluation: Based on the instinctive quality of drawing and the nuanced areas of grey in the background. (Photo on next page.)

Cathedrals

LESSON 106   Optical Mosaic   Beginning/Intermediate/Advanced

Purpose: To execute a paper mosaic in an optical expression.

Materials: Colored construction paper, pencils, newsprint, scissors, glue.

Procedure: Have students draw a preliminary sketch on newsprint (clown, flowers, landscape). Decide on colors to be used. Cut colored paper into ½″ squares. Proceed,
gluing bits of paper onto the drawing. This is similar to mosaics, except an area
should be limited to two colors in a repeat pattern. Each section should continue
the repeat design of two colors. The finished mosaic should present an optical
effect similar to optical painting.

Evaluation: Based on the optical effects and mosaic style.

LESSON 107   Crayon Impressionism   Beginning/Intermediate/Advanced

Purpose: To create an impressionistic expression with crayon.

Materials: Crayons, white drawing paper, still-life setup.

Procedure: Have students view a still-life setup and express the visual stimulus in impressionistic style. Using the points of colored crayons, pressure dots of color onto the white paper, referring to the still life as a guide. Be alert to warm and cool contrasts.

Evaluation: Based on the impressionistic appearance and total composition.

LESSON 108 Contour Drawing on Black Surface Beginning/Intermediate/Advanced

Purpose: To reverse the appearance of a contour line drawing.

Materials: Black construction paper, white conti crayon.

Procedure: Have a student model be the visual stimulus. Students should follow the same procedure as in any contour drawing assignment. The effect and appearance of the drawing will differ, as will the experience.

Evaluation: Based on the reverse appearance of the contour line.

LESSON 109 Self-Portrait Painting Beginning/Intermediate/Advanced

Purpose: To express one's personality in the form of a painting.

Materials: Pencils, white drawing paper, tempera paint, paint trays, water cups, brushes, mirrors.

Procedure: Have students position themselves in front of mirrors and draw their own images as they appear in the mirrors. After the drawings are complete, tempera paint is applied. Remind students to be alert to facial color change and details of facial structure. This is an excellent exercise challenge for future paintings. Suggest experimenting with various facial expressions.

Evaluation: Based on the painterly quality of the expression as well as the use of details and contrasting flesh tones. (Photo on next page.)

Hallie

LESSON 110   Pen and Ink Perspective   Beginning/Intermediate/Advanced

Purpose: To introduce simple perspective with a permanent medium.

Materials: Pencils, white drawing paper, india ink, pens, felt markers (optional).

Procedure: Have students draw on white drawing paper a series of simple buildings in two-point perspective. After drawing is complete, the entire drawing is rendered in pen and india ink. It is important to record recessive areas with darker shading and advancing areas with lighter application. Also be alert to details. Three-dimensional qualities should be expressed throughout the drawing.

　　　　　　　　If ink spillage or blots become a problem, have students use the more secure method of felt marker.

Evaluation: Based on the mastery of perspective as well as the proper and extensive use of pen-and-ink medium.

CHAPTER IV Three-Dimensional Activities

111. Papier-Mâché
112. Wood Construction
113. Wood Construction Relief
114. Wood Carved Relief
115. Wood Inlay
116. Wood Carving
117. Plaster Carving
118. Papier-Mâché Relief
119. Plaster Relief
120. Toothpick Relief
121. Wood Sculpture
122. Toothpick Construction
123. Toothpick Architecture
124. Linoleum Relief
125. Soap Carving
126. Sandcore Carving
127. Driftwood Carving
128. Straw Construction
129. Bark Relief
130. Bark Inlay
131. Bark Carving
132. Bark Construction
133. Cardboard Mobile
134. Styrofoam Sculpture
135. Styrofoam Carving
136. Straw Mobile
137. Straw Stabile
138. Reed Relief
139. Clay Modeling
140. Clay Tiles
141. Clay Carving
142. Foil Sculpture
143. Cork Inlay
144. Wire Sculpture
145. Wire Construction
146. Wire Hanging Sculpture
147. Egg Shell Optical Relief
148. Egg Shell Relief
149. Egg Carton Construction
150. Egg Carton Relief
151. Egg Shell Mosaic
152. Egg Carton Mural
153. Fabric Collage
154. Fabric Appliqué
155. Fabric Weaving
156. Tie and Dye
157. Felt Appliqué
158. Copper/Tin/Brass Tooling
159. Felt Modeling
160. Leaf Collage
161. Styrofoam Relief
162. Wood Architecture
163. Leather Mosaic
164. Leather Mural
165. Leather Relief
166. Linoleum Inlay
167. Spaghetti Sculpture
168. Styrofoam Relief
169. Cork Construction
170. Cork Relief

LESSON 111   **Papier-Mâché**   **Beginning/Intermediate/Advanced**

Purpose: To explore the use of common materials in a three-dimensional form.

Materials: Newspapers, scissors, wheat paste, water, water vat, tempera paint, paint trays, water cups, brushes, fixative or clear varnish, boxes, masking tape.

Procedure: Have students gather several boxes of various sizes. If animal-making is the assignment, have students choose a large box for the body, smaller boxes for legs, and even smaller boxes for the feet. Additional boxes are needed for the neck, head, and ears. Tape one box to another until the major parts of the body are all joined together.

Cut strips of newspaper. Pour wheat paste and water into a large vat or tub. Stir until creamy. Run strips of newsprint paper through the solution and carefully apply them to the animal form. Continue the process until the form is structurally sturdy. Allow to dry completely. Using tempera paint, apply color and textures throughout the animal form. After the form is satisfactorily painted, allow to dry. Finally, spray entire animal with fixative, or brush on clear varnish.

Evaluation: Based on ingenious use of animal form and three-dimensional design.

LESSON 112   **Wood Construction**   **Beginning/Intermediate/Advanced**

Purpose: To construct a three-dimensional abstract design with wood scraps.

Materials: Scraps of wood, glue, sandpaper.

Procedure: Have students select scraps of wood (generally available from school wood shop) which vary in size and shape. Have students glue pieces of wood in an upward direction, considering both the positive forms of the wood and the negative space surrounding the wood pieces. If necessary, wood pieces should be sanded before assembling.

Evaluation: Based on balance and distribution of positive and negative space.

LESSON 113   **Wood Construction Relief**   **Intermediate/Advanced**

Purpose: To construct with wood scraps a wood additive relief in architectural form.

Materials: Scraps of wood, glue, sandpaper, long wood panel or masonite.

Procedure: Have students select scraps of wood varying in size, shape, and color. Arranging the scraps on a long wood panel or masonite, students should consider the wood pieces as buildings or a landscape scene. After pieces are composed, considering placement and balance according to size, shape, and color, they are glued in place. Wood finishes can be applied before or after gluing. Stains should be applied to individual wood pieces before gluing.

Evaluation: Based on architectural appearance of the wood construction relief.

LESSON 114 Wood Carved Relief   Intermediate/Advanced

Purpose: To carve a relief design into wood or wood panel.

Materials: Wood (pine, cherry, maple), wood panel, pencils, drawing paper, X-acto knives, gouging knives.

Procedure: Have students draw preliminary sketches on paper, noting areas to be high or low relief. After transferring drawing to wood, carve out high-relief sections first. Then continue cutting until all high- and low-relief sections are cut out. Cut with grain of wood as much as possible. Design should be organized to match corresponding grain.

Evaluation: Based on high-, low-, or level-relief composition.

LESSON 115 Wood Inlay   Advanced

Purpose: To execute a design with various grains, colors, textures, and stains of wood, subtracting and adding materials.

Materials: Drawing paper, soft pine board, saber saw, drill, glue, wood scraps, pencils, stain.

Procedure: Have students draw an abstract design, using rectangular shapes, on drawing paper. Label shapes to be cut out. Transfer the drawing onto a pine board. Drill a hole into each section to be cut out. Using a saber saw, cut out the rectangular shapes. After all shapes are cut out, place the board over a second board of similar size, and glue down.

Cut matching rectangular shapes of different types, grains, colors, and textures of wood to fit into the original cut design. Staining of pieces should be done before setting in place.

Evaluation: Based on the unity of the composition in relation to the variety of shapes, colors, stains, and textures.

LESSON 116 Wood Carving   **Beginning/Intermediate/Advanced**

Purpose: To carve a head portrait in three-dimensional form.

Materials: Soft wood (6" x 10"), wood-carving tools, sandpaper, awls or razor blades, pencils, paper.

Procedure: Using a piece of soft wood, have students design a head, using all four sides of the wood. Begin carving with a sharp paring knife or wood-carving tool. Consider the three-dimensional qualities at all times. A preliminary drawing of a head in detail should act as a guide. Textures can be achieved with gouging tools. Sand other pieces or sections for proper effects.

Evaluation: Based on the strength of design evident from all four angles.

LESSON 117 Plaster Carving   **Beginning/Intermediate/Advanced**

Purpose: To execute a three-dimensional carving in a permanent medium. To express the recessive and advanced areas of a single color.

Materials: Plaster of Paris, half-gallon cardboard milk cartons or similar containers, water, water container, stirring paddle, carving knives, sponge, large cloths for wetting down plaster.

Procedure: Students should choose an appropriate carton to fit idea. Have students pour the proper amount of water into the water container. Plaster powder is then added, stirred until creamy, and poured immediately into cardboard carton. Allow to set overnight. When project stands idle, have it wrapped up tightly with wet rags. (If plaster should become too dry to carve, submerge completely in water for 24 hours.) After plaster has stood overnight, remove carton. Plaster is ready to carve. While they carve, have students consider all sides so that three dimensions sustain the image.

Evaluation: Based on the sculptural principle of viewing the object from all angles. (Photo on next page.)

Abstract

LESSON 118   Papier-Mâché Relief   Beginning/Intermediate/Advanced

Purpose: To execute in relief form an abstract, realistic, or architectural design.

Materials: Newspapers, paper cutter or scissors, heavy cardboard, wheat paste, water, water vat, pencils, white toweling.

Procedure: Have students draw an idea on heavy cardboard. Apply papier-mâché ingredients (wheat paste and water) to those areas of the drawing that are to be made three-dimensional. After this buildup is complete, run white toweling strips through the papier-mâché solution and apply to the entire relief, retaining the contour of shapes throughout. The consistency of white toweling will provide shadows and highlights. Allow to dry thoroughly before painting, if desired.

Evaluation: Based on the uniformity of design.

LESSON 119   Plaster Relief   Beginning/Intermediate/Advanced

Purpose: To execute a single-tone relief.

Materials: Plaster of Paris, water, two-gallon bucket, stirring paddle, plaster container, pencils, drawing paper, carving tools, sponge, several old rags.

Procedure: Have students draw a preliminary sketch of a still life or landscape. Then select a cardboard container to fit the size of the drawing. The cardboard container should be 2" or 3" deep to allow for deep gouging, if necessary.

Prepare plaster by pouring water into a two-gallon bucket, adding plaster of Paris, and stirring until a creamy substance is formed. Then pour into a cardboard mold or container. Allow sufficient time (4 to 8 hours) before peeling off the cardboard from the plaster. Once cardboard is removed, have students start the relief process by gouging out areas of negative space. The thicker the plaster, the deeper the gouge.

Evaluation: Based on the uniform composition and the three-dimensional effects of the relief.

LESSON 120   Toothpick Relief   Beginning/Intermediate/Advanced

Purpose: To execute a relief design through the additive method.

Materials: Masonite, tempera paint or enamel, toothpicks, glue, razor blades (optional).

Procedure: Have students first paint or enamel masonite, using one color or several colors to form an intricate pattern. Lay and glue rounded toothpicks onto the colored masonite, forming a flat pattern throughout. Once the design is established, additional toothpicks are glued atop the original ones to begin the relief form. Consider high and low relief patterns for variety. (Toothpicks should be arranged in vertical and horizontal directions; otherwise, confusion results.) Toothpicks can be cut with razor blades for smaller bits.

Evaluation: Based on the variety of highs and lows of the design, plus balance and unity of the composition.

LESSON 121   Wood Sculpture   Beginning/Intermediate/Advanced

Purpose: To execute a sculpture in wood through the additive method.

Materials: Wood pieces, sandpaper, wood cutting tools, glue, pencils, paper.

Procedure: Have students cut, shape, and carve pieces of wood representing sections of a whole. An idea should first be drawn on paper in a semi-realistic form. For example, a head can be made up of several parts: head, nose, lips, ears, eyes. Pieces of wood are cut and shaped to represent these parts. After all parts are shaped and sanded, glue them together. Details may be added by careful cutting into the finished product (eyes, lids, hair textures, etc.).

Evaluation: Based on the semi-realistic quality and possible emotional content.

LESSON 122   Toothpick Construction   Beginning/Intermediate/Advanced

Purpose: To execute an abstract linear design in three-dimensional form.

Materials: White toothpicks, fast-drying glue, wood base, nail or awl.

Procedure: Have students select a wood base appropriate to the design. Press a series of holes with a nail or awl into the top of the wood base. Apply glue to the toothpicks and place in holes in an upright position. Hold in place until the glue sets. Then apply toothpicks in succession in various directions to create interesting linear shapes. Continue this process until desired height and width are attained.

Evaluation: Based on the interweaving of linear positive and negative space.

LESSON 123   Toothpick Architecture   Beginning/Intermediate/Advanced

Purpose: To design an architectural setting of buildings.

Materials: Large base (pine, masonite), toothpicks, glue, nails, hammer, pencils, rulers, drawing paper.

Procedure: Have students draw a front view of a series of buildings (malls, neighborhoods, downtown) on paper. Redraw onto masonite or wood. At the four corners of each building, make slight openings with hammer and nail to allow for toothpicks to be positioned and glued. After all upright toothpicks are positioned and set in place tightly, add toothpicks horizontally across the vertical ones. Continue process until design is complete. Upward movement can continue until desired height is reached.

Evaluation: Based on the architectural appearance, balance, and composition.

LESSON 124   Linoleum Relief   Beginning/Intermediate/Advanced

Purpose: To execute a low-relief design from a dual-purpose material.

Materials: Linoleum, linoleum cutters, pencils, drawing paper, carbon paper, wood panel.

Procedure: Since linoleum basically serves printmaking, the cut itself can be used as a relief project. Have students draw the entire composition in pencil on drawing paper, labelling those areas to be in relief. Textured areas should also be considered. Trace drawing onto linoleum with carbon paper. Cut out the textured areas. When design is completely cut according to preliminary drawing, have relief mounted onto a wood panel for hanging.

Evaluation: Based on variety of textures, shapes, sizes, and balance of composition.

LESSON 125 Soap Carving   **Beginning/Intermediate/Advanced**

Purpose: To execute a three-dimensional expression from an easily carved material.

Materials: Bar of soap, paring knife, pencils, drawing paper, cloth.

Procedure: Have students draw a preliminary sketch of a simple animal form suitable for the soap shape to be carved. Working from the drawing, whittle away unnecessary areas. Cut thinly. Pieces that are too large result in breakage. It is best to cup soap in hands for better control. Carve as little as necessary to acquire three-dimensional qualities. Details can be carved by using the point of the knife. Rub with dry cloth for shiny results.

Evaluation: Based on the suitability of idea to material.

LESSON 126 Sandcore Carving   **Beginning/Intermediate/Advanced**

Purpose: To carve a three-dimensional object using the subtractive method.

Materials: Sandcore, paring knife, box or tray, sticks, pencils, drawing paper.

Procedure: Have students first draw on paper an idea suitable to the shape of the block of sand. (Sandcore can be secured from local foundries.) Using paring knife or any straight-edge tool (table knife, scissors, ruler), scrape away sand to first form a shape similar to the idea. Continue this process until the form emerges. Be careful not to overscrape. Details can be added with finer tools (compass point, needles). The student may wish to carve directly, allowing the shape of the sandcore to dictate the idea.

Evaluation: Based on the suitability of the idea to the material.

LESSON 127 Driftwood Carving   **Intermediate/Advanced**

Purpose: To use a natural object for sculptural purposes.

Materials: Pieces of driftwood, carving tools, wax polish, stains, cloth, sandpaper.

Procedure: From the shape and texture already present in the wood, have students carve a more definite shape. It helps if the driftwood is dry. Have students carve while holding wood in hands if the wood is soft. Otherwise, a vise may be necessary. Suggestive qualities of the wood generally enable students to define the shape more quickly. After the idea is defined and carved to satisfaction, finish with sandpaper for a smoother appearance. A final wax polish or stain will further enhance the wood.

Evaluation: Based on the finished product in relationship to the idea. (Photo on next page.)

Driftwood

LESSON 128   Straw Construction   **Beginning/Intermediate/Advanced**

Purpose: To construct a three-dimensional design with straws.

Materials: White straws, fast-drying glue, scissors or X-acto knife, wallboard or paneling.

Procedure: Have students make a construction by gluing straws together, parallel or at various angles to each other. Students can trim the straws as the design progresses. The finished construction can be attached to wallboard or paneling for an attractive wall plaque.

Evaluation: Based on the abstract distribution of positive and negative space.

LESSON 129 **Bark Relief**   **Intermediate/Advanced**

Purpose: To use a natural form in a three-dimensional design.

Materials: Pieces of bark, paring knife, glue, sandpaper, wood panel or wallboard, fine screws or panel pins (optional).

Procedure: Have students select pieces of bark of various shapes, colors, and textures. Break and trim them so they will lie flat. Glue the pieces of bark onto a wood panel or wallboard. Be sure the sections being glued are flat, so they remain permanently set in place. If the relief is to be a wall decoration, fine screws or panel pins can be used to attach the heavier pieces of bark.

Evaluation: Based on the overall composition of bark of various textures, colors, and shapes.

LESSON 130 **Bark Inlay**   **Intermediate/Advanced**

Purpose: To use natural forms in an artistic abstract design.

Materials: Wood board, panel pins or screws, glue, saw, bark pieces, delayed-setting plaster, spoon or knife.

Procedure: Have students select bark with deep textural ridges. Arrange the bark in a suitable design. Glue, pin, or screw in place on wood board or panel. Mix delayed-setting plaster and fill in between the ridges, using a spoon or knife. Fill in wherever necessary. The finished appearance should reflect the linear design of the plaster and the area design of the bark.

Evaluation: Based on the unified relationship between various types, colors, and shapes of bark.

LESSON 131 **Bark Carving**   **Beginning/Intermediate/Advanced**

Purpose: To use a natural form and transform it into apparent reality.

Materials: Pieces of bark, coping or hack saw, paring knife, sandpaper, glue, wooden base or panel.

Procedure: Have students select a large piece of bark suggesting a form of nature. Carve or saw away areas that interfere with the suggested form. Sandpaper the inside areas of bark if desirable. Glue the form to a wooden base for an upright sculpture, or to a wooden panel for a wall plaque.

Evaluation: Based on the suggestive quality of the form.

LESSON 132 **Bark Construction**   Beginning/Intermediate/Advanced

Purpose: To execute an abstract or semi-abstract three-dimensional form from nature.

Materials: Several pieces of bark (large and small), glue.

Procedure: Have students select several pieces of bark that can be used to form a complete construction. Variety of shapes and sizes and textures should be considered. Have pieces glued together. It may be necessary to glue small pieces to a large piece before gluing two heavier pieces.

Evaluation: Based on uniformity of design relative to textures, colors, sizes, and shapes.

LESSON 133 **Cardboard Mobile**   Beginning/Intermediate/Advanced

Purpose: To design various shapes and sizes of cardboard into a mobile.

Materials: Tempera paint, brushes, water cups, paint trays, scissors, pencils, drawing paper, white cardboard, string, glue, wire or dowels.

Procedure: Have students first select a natural object and expand it into a series of seven or more (for example, a fish, bird, or turtle). Have several variations drawn. Redraw onto white cardboard. Cut out and paint in a realistic or imaginative style on both sides of the cardboard. Allow to dry.

Cut several pieces of fine wire. Attach two designed objects to string or thread, which in turn is attached to the wire. The longer strings should be anchored by the larger designed pieces of cardboard for balance. After attaching two stringed objects to each piece of horizontal wire, attach the wires and add a final string to the center piece for hanging. If the three-dimensional mobile collapses, it must be balanced by varying the lengths of strings.

Evaluation: Based on balance of design and neatness of painted pieces.

LESSON 134 **Styrofoam Sculpture**   Beginning/Intermediate/Advanced

Purpose: To execute a three-dimensional form through the additive method.

Materials: Pieces of styrofoam, jig or band saw, file, glue, wood plaque or base, pencils, drawing paper.

Procedure: Have students select various sizes and shapes of white styrofoam. After students have drawn preliminary sketches of designs, have them cut shapes to correspond to designs. Glue in place. Styrofoam can be cut with band saw; more intricate pieces can be cut with jig saw. Design can be mounted on a wooden horizontal plaque or a vertical base.

Evaluation: Based on the unity of positive and negative space.

LESSON 135   **Styrofoam Carving**   **Intermediate/Advanced**

Purpose: To execute a three-dimensional sculptural form through the subtractive method.

Materials: Large piece of styrofoam, coping or hack saw, wood base or plaque, pencils, drawing paper.

Procedure: Working from a large vertical block of styrofoam, have students first draw a preliminary sketch indicating which sections should be cut out. Consider small, large, and narrow areas so that a variety of positive and negative areas exists. Because styrofoam is spongy, have students use a sharp coping saw or hack saw to subtract those areas representing negative space. After the desired shapes are cut away, have the sculpture mounted on a wood base or plaque.

Evaluation: Based on the unification of negative and positive aspects, and architectural appearance.

LESSON 136   **Straw Mobile**   **Beginning/Intermediate/Advanced**

Purpose: To join a series of miniature straw constructions into a three-dimensional mobile.

Materials: Straws, fast-drying glue, scissors, string or thread, fine wire, dowels.

Procedure: Have students make a series of small straw constructions, of similar shapes but various sizes. Attach string or thread to ends of dowels, varying lengths. Attach small straw constructions to shorter-length strings and larger constructions to longer strings. Make 5 to 7 such attachments. Construct as usual for a mobile.

Evaluation: Based on variety and total balance of the mobile.

LESSON 137   **Straw Stabile**   **Beginning/Intermediate/Advanced**

Purpose: To execute a linear three-dimensional design in space.

Materials: White straws, threads, glue, razor blades.

Procedure: Have students construct a three-dimensional project with straws by gluing them together into a linear composition in space. Cut straws into different lengths. After completion of the stabile, score a number of the straws with a razor blade and insert a colored thread. Weave the thread throughout the straws to combine the stabile with a second linear design. A squirt of glue into each scored straw will secure the thread more tightly.

Evaluation: Based on the unification of the white straws with the colored threads in a dual balance of linear design.

LESSON 138 Reed Relief   **Beginning/Intermediate/Advanced**

Purpose: To execute a linear-relief design.

Materials: Reeds, razor blade or X-acto knife, wallboard or panel, panel pins or finishing nails, hammer, pencils, drawing paper, water, water container.

Procedure: Have students draw a preliminary sketch of a single aspect of nature (for example, an animal, human figure, or insect) on white drawing paper. The reeds should be dampened in water before they are used. Then have students transpose the drawing idea onto a panel or wallboard, cutting the supple reeds to fit the design. Apply the reeds to the panel with panel pins or small finishing nails. Continue cutting and adding reeds until the design is complete. Remember, the reeds must not be dry when used.

Evaluation: Based on the linear construction of the design.

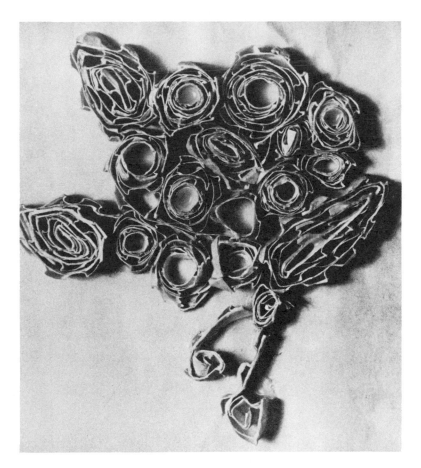

LESSON 139 Clay Modeling   **Beginning/Intermediate/Advanced**

Purpose: To model a flexible medium into a three-dimensional expression.

Materials: Prepared clay, looped-wire tool, spoon, fork.

Procedure: Have students shape the clay freely with their hands, adding or subtracting as the clay takes form. The handling of the clay may suggest an idea, or the student may work from a preliminary sketch. Keep the base of the clay fairly thick. Have students model the clay mostly with their hands; finer tools can be used later for details. As the outside shape takes form, have students remove clay from within the form with a spoon or looped-wire tool. This should be done before details are added. Make the walls of the clay form as thin as necessary for firing.

Evaluation: Based on realistic or imaginative portrayal.

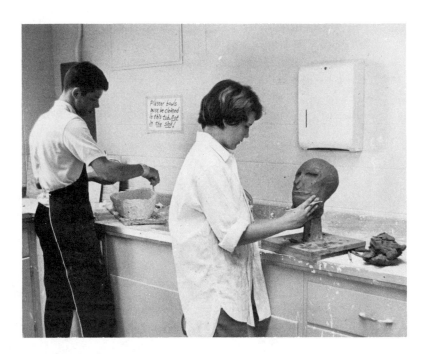

Clay Heads

LESSON 140   Clay Tiles   Beginning/Intermediate/Advanced

Purpose: To execute a tile relief with a simple flexible medium.

Materials: Prepared clay, sand, small tools (such as knife, spoon, paper clips, sticks, ruler), board, burlap or cloth, roller.

Procedure: Have students mix some coarse sand with the clay before starting in order to avoid having the tile warp as it dries. The clay should be rolled out onto a board covered with burlap or cloth to avoid clay sticking to the roller. Once the clay is rolled out evenly, impressions should be made in the moist clay with several tools. Abstract designs or semi-abstract patterns can be formed into a relief of different depths. After the design is complete, it can be left to dry as is, or it can be bisque-fired or glazed-fired.

Evaluation: Based on the overall pattern and the variations of shallow and deep indentations. If bisque-fired, variations of shadowy effects become a factor in evaluation. Glazed-firing will present other factors for evaluation.

LESSON 141   Clay Carving   Beginning/Intermediate/Advanced

Purpose: To carve a three-dimensional object from hardened clay.

Materials: Prepared clay, paring knife, compass point.

Procedure: Have students shape a suggestive form from prepared clay while it is still wet. Allow to dry to a leathery finish. Have students use a paring knife to carve away clay to a realistic form—an animal or a human head. Cut in details with the point of the paring knife or a compass point. Finally, chip textures or carve a linear design, if desired.

Evaluation: Based on realistic appearance from all angles.

LESSON 142   Foil Sculpture   Beginning/Intermediate/Advanced

Purpose: To model in three-dimensional form a semi-realistic expression from a common material.

Materials: Tin foil, scissors, glue.

Procedure: Have students crumple several layers of tin foil into a suggestive animal or head form. Continuously use fingers to press in areas where needed. Pull out other areas to suit the idea. If additional tin foil is needed, add to the shape, but glue may be necessary to keep it from unraveling from the original form. Continue this process until the desired effect is achieved.

Evaluation: Based on unity of the three-dimensional form as viewed from all angles.

LESSON 143   Cork Inlay   Beginning/Intermediate/Advanced

Purpose: To inlay a design with cork materials.

Materials: Two layers of ¼" cork, several pieces of colored cork, X-acto knife, glue, pencils.

Procedure: Use two slabs of cork ¼" thick (18" x 24"), each a different color. Have students draw an abstract design onto one of the slabs. With an X-acto knife, cut rectangular pieces of varying shapes and sizes out of the slab on which the drawing appears. After the design is completely cut, glue it in place over the second slab, which acts as a base. Trace the cutout cork pieces onto various colors of cork. Cut out with X-acto knife and place into the top layer of cork, fitting the cutout design. Watch for advancement of colors and textures.

Evaluation: Based on unity of design and interesting pattern of inlay.

LESSON 144   Wire Sculpture   Beginning/Intermediate/Advanced

Purpose: To construct a semi-realistic linear three-dimensional expression in wire.

Materials: Wire, pliers, wire cutters, brads or wire joints, wood base, pencils, drawing paper.

Procedure: Have students first draw a preliminary sketch of an animal or human figure. Bend picture-hanging wire into an abstract shape of an animal or a figure. After the outside body of the animal or figure is complete, use pliers to tighten more securely those wires that are loose. Reinforce with thinner wire wrapped around the point of connection. Once the contour of the object is established, finer wire is wrapped around the body. The more wire used, the more solid the object. After completion, mount on wood base with brads or wire joints.

Evaluation: Based on ingenuity of the idea and appearance of the object from all sides.

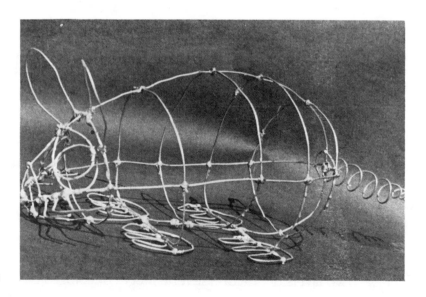

Mouse

LESSON 145 **Wire Construction** **Beginning/Intermediate/Advanced**

Purpose: To abstract a three-dimensional expression in linear form.

Materials: Wire, pliers, wire cutters, wood panel, brads.

Procedure: Have students bend fine wire into an abstract design considering spatial effects. Joints between one wired area and another are strengthened with additional wire. The contour effect should be sustained as much as possible. After completion, attach to wooden plaque or panel with brads or small nails for wall hanging.

Evaluation: Based on balance and unity of line and space, and the total abstract effect.

LESSON 146 **Wire Hanging Sculpture** **Beginning/Intermediate/Advanced**

Purpose: To execute a hanging wire design in space.

Materials: Wires, pliers, wire cutters, string.

Procedure: Have students proceed in the fashion used for wire construction. Students should consider location to determine the general shape of the project. Wire is kept linear during the process. The completed sculpture should be hung in front of a white or beige backdrop.

Evaluation: Based on the principles of three-dimensional sculpture in space.

LESSON 147 **Egg Shell Optical Relief** **Intermediate/Advanced**

Purpose: To execute a three-dimensional optical relief.

Materials: Several egg shells, small scissors, glue, egg carton (2½-dozen size), tempera paint, paint trays, water cups, small brushes.

Procedure: Have students use half egg shells, cleaning them and trimming with small scissors. Then glue the shells into the egg-container holes, with either end of the egg shells up. Paint the shells in a colorful optical fashion. If desired, the container can also be painted in an optical style.

Evaluation: Based on total optical effects in the three-dimensional design.

LESSON 148   **Egg Shell Relief**   **Beginning/Intermediate/Advanced**

Purpose: To execute a three-dimensional relief.

Materials: Several egg shells, small scissors, glue, egg carton (2½-dozen size), tempera paint, paint trays, water cups, small brushes.

Procedure: Have students use half egg shells, cleaning them and trimming with small scissors. Then glue the shells into the egg-container holes. The egg composition should be determined before gluing. Some egg holes can be left empty, while others can have shells glued side by side. The remaining space in the cardboard container may be painted white. This will cause some exciting shadows between the various egg shells and the negative counterparts. When complete, the relief can be displayed as a wall hanging or wall plaque.

Evaluation: Based on the total positive and negative effects of the white egg shells and the white background.

LESSON 149   **Egg Carton Construction**   **Beginning/Intermediate/Advanced**

Purpose: To execute a three-dimensional sculptural construction through the additive method.

Materials: Various sized egg cartons, scissors, glue, wooden base or plaque.

Procedure: Have students select egg cartons of several different sizes. Using glue, stick the side of one egg carton to the side of another. Continue the process until desired height and direction are achieved, considering balance at all times. The construction can be displayed as a hanging, stabile, or projection.

Evaluation: Based on unity of design and total composition.

LESSON 150   **Egg Carton Relief**   **Beginning/Intermediate/Advanced**

Purpose: To execute an architectural design in relief.

Materials: Egg cartons of different sizes and shapes, glue, scissors, wood base or panel.

Procedure: Have students gather several egg cartons ranging in size from ½ dozen to 2½ dozen, and arrange them in architectural fashion onto plywood or paneling. Egg cartons can be used inward or outward for variety. After arrangement is complete, students can glue cartons in place. Stand cartons on a mantel or hang them on a wall.

Evaluation: Based on total unity of design in relation to balance.

LESSON 151   Egg Shell Mosaic   Beginning/Intermediate/Advanced

Purpose: To create a mosaic design with common material.

Materials: Colored egg shells, small mallet, glue, wallboard, pencils.

Procedure: Have students draw design directly onto piece of wallboard. Dye several egg shells, allowing them to dry. Break them into small bits. Glue into place onto the wallboard design, allowing narrow slits of white wallboard to separate each small piece. Be alert to contrasting shapes so that the design sustains itself.

Evaluation: Based on the total unity of design.

LESSON 152   Egg Carton Mural   Intermediate/Advanced

Purpose: To decorate a large wall of a school or community building.

Materials: Convenient wall (preferably wood, cork or panel), glue, various egg cartons of different shapes and sizes, scissors, X-acto knives, pencils, drawing paper.

Procedure: Have students draw preliminary sketches of ideas to be used for the mural. Redraw design onto wall. Cut and trim egg cartons and glue into position on the mural wall. Vary design by inverting some of the cartons.

Evaluation: Based on the architectural appearance of the mural.

LESSON 153   Fabric Collage   Beginning/Intermediate/Advanced

Purpose: To execute a collage expression with scraps of various cloths.

Materials: Colored burlap, scissors, glue; various scraps of cloth of different colors, shapes, sizes, and textures; pencils, drawing paper, small objects (sequins, buttons, cotton, etc.).

Procedure: Have students draw preliminary sketch on paper. Refer to drawing while gluing scraps of cloth onto the colored burlap. Add other materials such as sequins, buttons, and cotton.

Evaluation: Based on the sophisticated use of various materials and objects.

LESSON 154   **Fabric Appliqué**   **Beginning/Intermediate/Advanced**

Purpose: To sew fabrics onto burlap in an imaginative design.

Materials: Different types, colors, and textures of fabrics; scissors, needles, threads, burlap, panel of wood, staples.

Procedure: Have students cut shapes from different fabrics and arrange them into a design. Have another piece of cloth or burlap cut large enough to hold the design. Keep the burlap flat and taut while the various pieces of fabric are sewn onto the burlap. When complete, have the design stapled onto the panel of wood.

Evaluation: Based on the unification of the various types, textures, and colors of the fabrics.

LESSON 155   **Fabric Weaving**   **Beginning/Intermediate/Advanced**

Purpose: To weave a fabric without a loom.

Materials: Small weights, selection of various fabrics, safety pins, threads, needles, netting, mesh, or burlap.

Procedure: Have students select mesh, burlap, or netting, and hang it vertically with weights for tautness. Then cut different kinds of fabric into long thin strips. Using a safety pin, weave the strips across the netting into a pattern or design. To prevent slipping of strips, catch ends with a stitch or two.

Evaluation: Based on the complexity of design and overall composition.

LESSON 156   **Tie and Dye**   **Beginning/Intermediate/Advanced**

Purpose: To execute the tie-and-dye method of design.

Materials: White cotton cloth, thread, scissors, dyes.

Procedure: Have students use any plain white cotton fabric, bunching up and tying certain areas of the cloth to be dipped into the dye. The parts of the cloth tied will repel the dye and remain white. Keep the tied part of the cloth dipped until the dye takes effect. After allotted time, remove the thread or string holding the bunched cloth together. Bunch and dip other sections until desired effects are achieved. After the cloth is dry, wash and iron it.

Evaluation: Based on colorful design and uniformity of composition.

LESSON 157   Felt Appliqué   Beginning/Intermediate/Advanced

Purpose: To do a felt appliqué in abstract design.

Materials: Colored felt, scissors, needle, thread, frame, staple gun, fabric.

Procedure: Have students cut different colored pieces of felt into various shapes and sizes. Stretch a second piece of fabric over a wooden frame, turning the edges over and stapling them to the back. The edges should be pulled tight, with crossing stitches at the back. Arrange the felt shapes onto the fabric and sew in place. The design need not be abstract.

Evaluation: Based on the unification and total composition of the design.

LESSON 158   Copper/Tin/Brass Tooling   Beginning/Intermediate/Advanced

Purpose: To execute a relief form of expression.

Materials: Copper, brass, or tin foil, pencils, drawing paper, tracing paper, newspapers, tooling devices, brush, liver of sulphur, wooden panel, cloth.

Procedure: Have students draw a preliminary sketch on drawing paper to the size of the copper, brass, or tin-foil sheet. Trace drawing onto sheet. Invert design onto pad of newspaper. Using spoon or similar tool, press down on those areas of design to be depressed. Push other areas out until design is satisfactory. Brush on a coat of liver of sulphur. Allow to dry, and rub down with soft cloth for highlights. Recessive areas should sustain the antique color of the sulphur solution.

Evaluation: Based on the relief effect and the appropriateness of the idea. (Photo on page 80.)

LESSON 159   Felt Modeling   Beginning/Intermediate/Advanced

Purpose: To make a simple three-dimensional figure from a simple material.

Materials: Pencils, drawing paper, scissors, thread, needle, bits of colored felt, cotton balls.

Procedure: Have students draw a picture of a simple figure. Consider the shapes of its different sides and make a sewing pattern for them. Remember to allow extra at the edges for turning in. Cut the side panels out of colored felt and sew them with a running stitch, allowing one panel to remain open. Turn the figure inside out and pack it with cotton balls. Sew up the last panel. Additional materials may be glued on, such as buttons or sequins.

Evaluation: Based on the figure's personality and the three-dimensional effects.

80

Copper/Tin/Brass Tooling
(Lesson 158)

LESSON 160   Leaf Collage   Beginning/Intermediate/Advanced

Purpose: To create a leaf collage expression.

Materials: Different sizes, shapes, types, and colors of leaves; glue, colored tissue paper, heavy colored cardboard, clear varnish, brush.

Procedure: Have students arrange leaves into a design, using the various types, sizes, colors, and shapes. Glue them onto a stable colored background. Leaves must be flat in order to adhere. After the design is complete, a different effect is achieved with an overlay of a colored piece of tissue paper. Apply clear varnish carefully over the tissue paper and allow to dry.

Evaluation: Based on the attractive appearance of the design, and the total composition.

LESSON 161 Styrofoam Relief   Beginning/Intermediate/Advanced

Purpose: To execute a relief using additive and subtractive methods.

Materials: Styrofoam slab, pencils, paper, glue, X-acto knife.

Procedure: Have students first draw a preliminary sketch on paper. Transfer drawing to styrofoam slab. Using an X-acto knife, cut away those areas to be depressed. Be sure all areas are rectangular. Cutout areas may be glued onto the slab, making a deeper relief.

Evaluation: Based on the complexity of design and variety of relief.

LESSON 162 Wood Architecture   Intermediate/Advanced

Purpose: To construct a three-dimensional model of a city.

Materials: Wood scraps, panel, glue, sandpaper.

Procedure: Have students select various sizes, colors, and textures of rectangular wood pieces. Plan layout of city on wood panel. After selecting appropriate wood pieces, glue them onto wood panel. Add pieces upward and laterally until "city" is complete. This will be a three-dimensional standing form of architecture. Smaller pieces can be cut for window and door attachments.

Evaluation: Based on the total complexity of design and composition.

LESSON 163 Leather Mosaic   Beginning/Intermediate/Advanced

Purpose: To create a mosaic from several colors and textures of leather.

Materials: Leather scraps, glue, a large skein of leather, scissors, pencils, drawing paper.

Procedure: Have students draw a preliminary sketch on drawing paper. Transfer drawing onto leather skein. Using different colors of leather, cut small rectangular shapes and glue onto the design, creating a mosaic-like appearance. Black leather can be used as the background skein to separate the leather bits.

Evaluation: Based on the mosaic-like appearance.

LESSON 164   Leather Mural   Intermediate/Advanced

Purpose: To execute a mural suitable for a school or community-building wall.

Materials: Large piece of plywood, masonite, or wallboard; glue or staple gun, large scraps of colored leather, charcoal or chalk, large drawing paper, scissors.

Procedure: Have students first draw a preliminary sketch suitable for a mural for community use. The paper should be as large as the proposed mural. Cut out the design and trace it onto plywood or masonite. Trace the pieces of cut paper onto the appropriate pieces of colored leather. After the design is completely cut, glue leather pieces onto the masonite or plywood. A staple gun may do the job more securely. Be sure that contrasting shapes are evident. Remember, the mural must be viewed from a distance.

Evaluation: Based on the strength of the mural and the total composition.

LESSON 165   Leather Relief   Intermediate/Advanced

Purpose: To execute the inlay method with various colors of leather.

Materials: Leather (large shank), scraps of colored leather, scissors, staple gun, X-acto knives, glue, pencils, drawing paper, panel or board.

Procedure: Working from a visual stimulus (still life, landscape, posed figures), have students draw a preliminary sketch on drawing paper. Staple leather shank to panel, wood, masonite, or drywall board. Transfer drawing onto leather shank. Using X-acto knives, cut particles out of leather drawing and redraw particles onto different-colored leather pieces. Put these pieces in place of those originally cut out. Glue in place.

Evaluation: Based on variety and arrangement of colors of leather, and total composition.

LESSON 166 **Linoleum Inlay**   **Beginning/Intermediate/Advanced**

Purpose: To execute an inlay method of expression with linoleum.

Materials: Large sheet of leather, glue, X-acto knives, colored linoleum scraps, pencils, drawing paper.

Procedure: Have students draw a preliminary sketch from visual stimulus. Transfer the drawing onto leather. Cut out pieces as in leather relief. However, cut deep enough to meet the underlying weave design. Retrace the cut pieces onto the colored pieces of linoleum and glue them into the open spaces already cut out. Be alert to balance of color and texture.

Evaluation: Based on total unification of composition.

LESSON 167 **Spaghetti Sculpture**   **Beginning/Intermediate/Advanced**

Purpose: To use a commercial product for three-dimensional effect.

Materials: Various lengths, widths, and thicknesses of spaghetti; fast-drying glue, wood base, nails, hammers.

Procedure: Have students pierce the wood base with a series of nail holes. Glue the ends of dried spaghetti in the nail holes. Continue to add to and build up the construction with various lengths and widths of spaghetti. Continue the process until desired height of the sculpture is achieved.

Evaluation: Based on distribution of line and space within the sculpture.

LESSON 168 **Styrofoam Relief**   **Beginning/Intermediate/Advanced**

Purpose: To execute a three-dimensional relief using additive and subtractive methods.

Materials: Styrofoam slab, X-acto knives, glue, pencils, drawing paper.

Procedure: Have students first prepare preliminary sketch. After transferring design onto styrofoam slab, cut away rectangular shapes with X-acto knives according to the design. The cutout shapes should then be glued to the slab as a part of the design to add to the height of the relief. This process is both subtractive and additive.

Evaluation: Based on depth and variety of relief and total composition.

LESSON 169   Cork Construction   **Beginning/Intermediate/Advanced**

Purpose: To create a three-dimensional construction using the additive method.

Materials: Cork scraps, glue, wood base, fine wire, drills.

Procedure: Have students glue together several natural pieces of cork, forming a standing sculpture. If glue doesn't work, drill holes and insert wires to hold the pieces together. This construction can hang, stand, or be a plaque.

Evaluation: Based on the uniformity of composition and structure.

LESSON 170   Cork Relief   **Beginning/Intermediate/Advanced**

Purpose: To execute a relief in three-dimensional form, either additive or subtractive or both.

Materials: Pencils, drawing paper, cork slab, scraps of cork, glue, X-acto knives.

Procedure: Have students first draw a preliminary sketch on drawing paper. Have them work from a visual stimulus, such as a still life. Redraw the sketch onto the cork slab. Whittle the scraps of cork down to fit the contour of the drawing. It helps if some cork bits of different colors are used. Glue into place, building up three-dimensional effects. Students can also subtract by cutting away segments of the cork slab.

Evaluation: Based on the unity of recessive and advancing segments of the relief.

CHAPTER V SPUR-OF-THE-MOMENT ACTIVITIES ■■■■

171. Limitation
172. Situation
173. Crowd of People
174. The Garbage Can
175. Bus Ride
176. Aging
177. Billboard
178. Losing the State Championship
179. Winning the State Championship
180. Four Seasons
181. Situation Ball Game
182. Games/Sporting Events
183. Neighborhood
184. Modes of Transportation
185. License Plate
186. City of Tomorrow
187. Hero Worship
188. If I Were President...
189. Perfume Ad
190. Sorrow and Hope
191. Happy Event
192. Inside of Room
193. Protest March
194. Inside-Outside
195. Family
196. Construction
197. Angle from Underneath
198. Angle from Overhead
199. Peephole
200. Embarrassing Moment
201. Birth and Death
202. The Funeral
203. The Wedding
204. Graduation
205. Job Interview
206. Talent Show
207. Dining Out
208. A Restless Night

209. Popcorn Factory
210. Drive-in Theater
211. Waiting at the Airport
212. Senior Prom
213. Cafeteria Line
214. The Clown
215. Supermarket Check-out
216. The Bread Line
217. Day at the Circus
218. Haunted House
219. Third World War
220. Working in a Bakery
221. The Fire Alarm
222. Political Campaign
223. Loneliness
224. Happiness
225. Love
226. Hate
227. Limitation Using a Holiday Theme
228. Band Practice
229. The Whistle Blew
230. Series of Blown Whistles
231. Taxi, Please!
232. A Day at the Races
233. The Picket Line
234. The Corner Newsstand
235. The Post Office at Christmas Time
236. City Dump
237. The Rescue
238. The Fire Plug
239. The Flood
240. The Park Bench
241. The Pet Show
242. Sunday Picnic
243. Trash Pickup
244. The Car Wash
245. The Dog Fight

(Note: These activities should all be done in a limited time frame—one hour, or one class period.)

LESSON 171   Limitation   **Beginning/Intermediate/Advanced**

Purpose: To test the imagination and mental resources within a limited proposal.

Materials: Pencils, white paper (9" x 12").

Procedure: Have students draw in a single picture the following objects: one church, one house, one fence, two trees, four flowers, one animal, and one mode of transportation. Draw no more, no less. Horizontal line is optional.

Evaluation: Based entirely on the unusual use and arrangement of the objects, or the angle from which they are viewed.

LESSON 172   Situation   **Beginning/Intermediate/Advanced**

Purpose: To test reactions to a common situation or experience.

Materials: Pencils, white paper (9" x 12").

Procedure: Have students draw in a single picture the following sentence: "While watching television one night, I heard a strange noise."

Evaluation: Based on the angle from which the television is viewed, and the unusual manner in which night is portrayed and the noise expressed. Judgment is based on the effect or damage of the noise.

LESSON 173   Crowd of People   **Beginning/Intermediate/Advanced**

Purpose: To do an illustration of a crowd of people.

Materials: Pencils, white paper (9" x 12").

Procedure: Have students draw six heads facing front near the bottom of the paper. Draw a different facial expression in each of the six heads. Add heads in the background, leading to the top of the paper. Heads should be attached to each other, with none hanging in space.

Evaluation: Based on accuracy and emotional content of the six facial expressions, as well as the illusion of a crowd. Any additional identifying factors regarding the crowd are also items for evaluation.

Crowd of People

LESSON 174   The Garbage Can   Beginning/Intermediate/Advanced

Purpose: To create a social commentary from a portrayal of a single object.

Materials: Pencils, white paper (9" x 12").

Procedure: Have students draw a garbage can in a single picture. Leftover space must be considered as the location of the can. Therefore, a background is included. Garbage can may be empty, full, or overflowing. Trash may be strewn outside the can. The garbage itself (cans, food scraps, bottles, packages) can be identified as to contents and names.

Evaluation: Based on the type of social commentary and the convincing manner in which it is portrayed. Also based on unusual arrangement and choice of garbage items.

(Photo on page 88.)

Garbage Can

LESSON 175   Bus Ride   Beginning/Intermediate/Advanced

Purpose: To exploit the creative potential of a single activity within a given time limit.

Materials: Pencils, white paper (9" x 12").

Procedure: Have students draw a bus ride in a single picture. Emphasize the negative aspect. Do not mention the type of bus or whether the inside or outside of the bus should be drawn. These choices are up to the students. If time allows, students should always give drawings a finished look (contrast, shading, textures, details).

Evaluation: Based on the unusual quality of the bus ride. Bus empty except for driver, close-up view of passengers, close-up view of bus, angle from which bus is drawn, any surprise element. Also based on arrangement or composition of the idea.

LESSON 176   Aging   Beginning/Intermediate/Advanced

Purpose: To express within a single picture and a limited time frame a sequence of human beings bearing witness to each other.

Materials: Pencils, white paper (9" x 12").

Procedure: Have students draw in a single picture four heads or figures, each representing a different stage of growth (young childhood, teenager, middle age, old age). Suggest a story connection between the four age groups. A background defining location should be added.

Evaluation: Based on the sequential manner of display. A definite relationship between the four stages of growth should be shown, as well as similarities or differences. Judgment is also made on the appropriate characteristics present within each of the four personalities.

LESSON 177   Billboard   Beginning/Intermediate/Advanced

Purpose: To test the imagination and prior knowledge of spatial relationships.

Materials: Pencils, white paper (9" x 12").

Procedure: Have students draw the view of a billboard at a particular distance, the largeness of the billboard determining the distance at which it is situated. Included on the billboard should be the location, type of services/business rendered, and hours of service.

Evaluation: Based on clarity of directions, unusual angle from which billboard is displayed, and unusual setting. Based also on contrast, perspective, textures, and details.

LESSON 178   Losing the State Championship   Beginning/Intermediate/Advanced

Purpose: To express the effect of a losing team.

Materials: Pencils, white paper (9" x 12").

Procedure: Have students draw in a single picture the effects of a team losing the state championship. Illustrate with facial expressions of the coach, players, schoolmates, and people of the community. No mention is made of the activity to be drawn. Suggest to students that the state championship may refer to anything from marbles to ping-pong to football to basketball.

Evaluation: Based on originality of composition and the degree to which its emotional content is convincing.

LESSON 179   Winning the State Championship   Beginning/Intermediate/Advanced

Purpose: To express the effect of winning the state championship.

Materials: Pencils, white paper (9" x 12").

Procedure: Have students draw in a single picture the effects that winning the state championship has upon the personalities involved (coach, players, school, community). Have students consider facial expressions as the major way to show the emotional traits of those affected.

Evaluation: Based on originality of composition and convincing emotional content.

LESSON 180   **Four Seasons**   **Beginning/Intermediate/Advanced**

Purpose: To express in a single picture four stages of seasonal change.

Materials: Pencils, white paper (9" x 12").

Procedure: Have students draw in a single picture the four seasonal changes of the year. The changes should reflect continuity rather than isolation. Ideas could involve such things as trees, flowers, or animals. Since color is not used, students should consider the effects of seasonal change on the shape of the object.

Evaluation: Based on imaginative choice of objects and arrangement in relation to background. Also based on recessive and advancing qualities of the altered objects.

LESSON 181   **Situation Ball Game**   **Beginning/Intermediate/Advanced**

Purpose: To express in a limited time frame a reaction to a given situation.

Materials: Pencils, white paper (9" x 12").

Procedure: Have students draw their reactions to the following sentence: "While I was sitting in the bleacher section watching the ball game, I was disturbed by an unusual commotion." Have students consider the items to be drawn (bleachers, ball game, commotion) and the arrangement necessary to incorporate them. Mention nothing of the kind of ball game. This opens up wide the possibilities of expression. The commotion itself is the most important, together with the manner in which it is portrayed (whether close-up or at a distance).

Evaluation: Based on the commotion and the reaction to it. Always, of course, consider perspective, details, textures, and contrast in relation to the whole.

LESSON 182   **Games/Sporting Events**   **Beginning/Intermediate/Advanced**

Purpose: To incorporate a number of games and/or sporting events into a single picture, reflecting several activities simultaneously.

Materials: Pencils, white paper (9" x 12").

Procedure: Have students draw into a single picture at least 10-15 different games or sporting events. You might suggest a division of three planes so that events can be relegated to each of three areas: sky (plane acrobatics, parachuting), land (baseball, skateboarding, roller skating), water (skiing, boating, fishing, swimming). Suggest a combination of games (hopscotch, marbles, chess) and sporting events (football, softball). The number of activities must make sense as to season as well as composition. Remember, this is to be a single expression composed of several ideas, and there is a time limit of one class period.

Evaluation: Based on the arrangement of the games and sports in perspective, the unusual choice of events, and the angle from which the events are viewed.

LESSON 183   Neighborhood   Beginning/Intermediate/Advanced

Purpose: To reveal in a single expression the various angles of an object within a given time frame.

Materials: Pencils, white paper (9" x 12").

Procedure: Have students draw in a single picture at least four houses, reflecting a neighborhood. Each house must be drawn from a different angle: one house from the back, one house from the front, one house from the side, and one from a three-quarter view, showing either front and side or back and side. The drawing must resemble a typical neighborhood. If time allows, have students texture each house differently, using wood, brick, stone, and stucco. The houses should be shown three-dimensionally. The picture may include additional objects.

Evaluation: Based on the convincing arrangement of houses as well as the neighborhood appearance. Also based on the use of perspective principles of receding and advancing objects.

LESSON 184   Modes of Transportation   Beginning/Intermediate/Advanced

Purpose: To test compositional powers with a given situation within a given time frame.

Materials: Pencils, white paper (9" x 12").

Procedure: Have students draw in a single picture a number of modes of transportation (10, 15, or 20, depending on the type of class). Each mode (train, boat, car, skateboard, etc.) must be an integral part of the picture. There should be a common-sense attitude or story-type sequence in the picture. People need not be drawn.

Evaluation: Based on the variety of modes of transportation and their unusual use. Based also on the degree of recessive and advancing qualities of the background planes, and again, details, textures, accents, and contrast in relation to the whole.

LESSON 185   License Plate   Beginning/Intermediate/Advanced

Purpose: To design a license plate within a given time frame.

Materials: Pencils, white paper (9" x 12").

Procedure: Have students draw a close-up view of a license plate. To be included on the plate are the plate number, year, name of state, nickname of state, and type of vehicle the plate is attached to. Beyond those instructions, nothing more should be said.

Evaluation: Based on the practical layout, appropriate relationship of state name to nick-name, and simplicity of lettering.

LESSON 186 City of Tomorrow   **Beginning/Intermediate/Advanced**

Purpose: To explore the possibilities of constructing a city of the future during a time unit of one class period.

Materials: Pencils, white paper (9" x 12").

Procedure: Have students draw as a single expression a view of a city of tomorrow. They should consider modes of transportation, living quarters, and type of landscape. (Don't be surprised if the city of tomorrow becomes an image of total destruc-tion.)

Evaluation: Based on creative imagination and projection of the central idea. Also based on composition relative to advancement and recession of objects and on details that relate to the whole.

LESSON 187 Hero Worship   **Beginning/Intermediate/Advanced**

Purpose: To express a reaction to current heroes in the form of a drawing.

Materials: Pencils, white paper (9" x 12").

Procedure: Have students draw in a single picture their reactions to a current hero or group of heroes, or portray themselves as heroes. Have them illustrate the type of hero, somehow identifying the activity that made the hero famous. A close-up view of the hero would be best, with the background as the identity factor.

Evaluation: Based on the convincing manner of expression and the reinforcement value of the accompanying background. Also based on the total composition in terms of contrast, texture, and details.

LESSON 188   **If I Were President...**   Beginning/Intermediate/Advanced

Purpose: To project in the form of a drawing ideas about the future in relation to the past.

Materials: Pencils, white paper (9" x 12").

Procedure: Have students draw in a single picture changes they would try to make if they were President of the United States. Encourage students to draw the single most significant change, which would enhance the lives of all Americans. Any related changes should also be considered.

Evaluation: Based on the convincing manner of expression and the practicality of the solutions to current problems.

LESSON 189   **Perfume Ad**   Beginning/Intermediate/Advanced

Purpose: To test the imagination for a fast layout of an ad for future production.

Materials: Pencils, white paper (9" x 12").

Procedure: Have students develop a layout of a perfume ad. Ad must include type of product (what is it?) and its name. Lettering should characterize the nature of the product. Since perfume is a feminine product, the layout should emphasize feminine traits.

Evaluation: Based on general design of the product and suitability of lettering to its name. Also based on composition and simplicity.

LESSON 190   **Sorrow and Hope**   Beginning/Intermediate/Advanced

Purpose: To express a form of sorrow and forthcoming hope in a single picture executed in a limited time frame.

Materials: Pencils, white paper (9" x 12").

Procedure: Have students draw in a single picture two emotional states: sorrow and hope. Students should consider forms of disaster or loss (human, animal, property), the effects upon those involved, and the hope of survival. Such events as fires, accidents, floods, strikes, layoffs, disease, and droughts are possibilities. Hope may be in the form of rescue squads, ambulances, doctor, nurse, fire fighter, and police officer. Suggest a close-up view rather than the usual objective approach.

Evaluation: Based on arrangement of ideas, convincing expressions of emotional reactions, angle from which the tragedy is portrayed, and details related to the entire composition.

LESSON 191   **Happy Event**   Beginning/Intermediate/Advanced

Purpose: To execute in the form of a drawing an emotional state of joy and the event leading up to it.

Materials: Pencils, white paper (9" x 12").

Procedure: Have students draw an expression of a happy event. Suggest a close-up view of the happening, with background reserved for related activities. Emphasize that people need not be drawn. In fact, a greater challenge exists without the presence of people at the event. Remember to emphasize limitation of time to one class period.

Evaluation: Based on effectiveness of emotional expression and arrangement and details of composition.

LESSON 192   **Inside of Room**   Beginning/Intermediate/Advanced

Purpose: To test knowledge of perspective and recall of objects.

Materials: Pencils, white paper (9" x 12").

Procedure: Have students draw a rectangle (any size) onto white drawing paper. The size shape, and position of the rectangle determine the interior of the room. Decide on type of room (such as bedroom, kitchen, den, or living room). After drawing the rectangle, extend its corners to the four corners of the paper. This will establish the ceiling, floor, back wall and two side walls. Choose two walls and place five objects on each. Add five objects to the floor and five to the ceiling. The result: an interior of a room furnished with a total of twenty objects.

Evaluation: Based on choice and placement of objects. Also based on perspective.

LESSON 193   **Protest March**   Beginning/Intermediate/Advanced

Purpose: To update activities warranting a protest march, and to enliven the spirit.

Materials: Pencils, white paper (9" x 12").

Procedure: Have students draw in a single picture a crowd or group of people marching for a cause. Vary facial expressions and identify type of clothing worn by the marchers. Signs carried by the protesters should be a significant part of the proceedings. A greater challenge might come from showing only the preparation or the aftermath of such an event.

Evaluation: Based on the actual purpose of the march, the portrayal of those involved, and the angle from which the march has been drawn.

LESSON 194   Inside-Outside   Beginning/Intermediate/Advanced

Purpose: To exhibit both the inside and the outside of a building or object in a single picture.

Materials: Pencils, white paper (9″ x 12″).

Procedure: Have students draw in a single picture the inside and the outside of a given building or mode of transportation (car, bus, train). A window is the best means of revealing what is inside. Showing the side of a building surrounding a window enables an inside activity as well as an outside event to be illustrated. The same holds true of a car, bus, or train. Remember that a time limit is necessary. The picture must retain a sense of proper composition. This preliminary test would serve well for a future painting.

Evaluation: Based on the type of activity, both indoor and out, and on proper perspective.

LESSON 195   Family   Beginning/Intermediate/Advanced

Purpose: To draw a response to a single title within a limited time frame.

Materials: Pencils, white paper (9″ x 12″).

Procedure: Have students draw in a single picture a family of human beings, animals, plants, or insects (such as a school of fish, a swarm of bees, a herd of elephants, a pack of wolves). Variety and arrangement are important, as are textures. In the case of the human family, ages become important.

Evaluation: Based on positioning of family in the total composition. Also based on variety, textures, accents, contrast, and details.

LESSON 196   Construction   Beginning/Intermediate/Advanced

Purpose: To record levels of construction of a particular building, composed in such a way as to indicate a sequence.

Materials: Pencils, white paper (9″ x 12″).

Procedure: Have students draw in a single picture three stages of construction of a single building (house, church, skyscraper). The stages may be a skeleton frame, enclosed frame, finished frame, or a hole in the ground; the building may be finished or razed. It should read like a 1-2-3 how-to-do-it picture.

Evaluation: Based on composition of the buildings, details involved, and the angle from which the buildings are drawn.

LESSON 197   Angle from Underneath   Beginning/Intermediate/Advanced

Purpose: To express a view from an unusual angle in a single picture and within a limited time frame.

Materials: Pencils, white paper (9" x 12").

Procedure: Have students draw in a single picture a view from underneath (for example, lying underneath a tree and looking up through the branches). The student must visualize himself or herself looking upward (city, skyscraper, elevator shaft, ceiling) and record what is seen from the unusual angle. Distortion will become a major part of the drawing.

Evaluation: Based on the distortion stemming from the angle being portrayed. Also based on three-dimensional effects, recessive and advancing qualities, and uniform composition.

LESSON 198   Angle from Overhead   Beginning/Intermediate/Advanced

Purpose: To express a view from the top looking downward, in a single picture within a limited time frame.

Materials: Pencils, white paper (9" x 12").

Procedure: Have students visualize being on a height looking downward, and then draw the vision. Examples would be looking down from an airplane, from a tall building, from the roof of a house, or from a treetop. Have students consider the abstract appearance that unusual viewpoints create. Also consider the time limit.

Evaluation: Based on the unusual portrayal of a natural scene, with distortion evident. Also based on all other fundamentals.

LESSON 199   Peephole   **Beginning/Intermediate/Advanced**

Purpose: To reflect an object or scene as it appears through a hole, slit, or slot.

Materials: Pencils, white paper (9" x 12").

Procedure: Have students draw something as it appears through a hole, slit, or slot. In order for the drawing to reflect both the inside and the outside, the border or surrounding area of the hole, slit, or slot should be drawn as the background area. The inside portrayal may use recessive qualities or a close-up depending on the student's choice. Examples would be a keyhole, transom opening, door opening, small window, periscope, telescope, or binoculars.

Evaluation: Based on the detailed study of the inner objects as seen through the openings. Also based on the surrounding area and the identity of the object through which the observation is being made.

LESSON 200   Embarrassing Moment   **Beginning/Intermediate/Advanced**

Purpose: To express in a single picture a moment of embarrassment using, if necessary, personal symbols.

Materials: Pencils, white paper (9" x 12").

Procedure: Have students draw an embarrassing moment on paper. Since this drawing hinges on embarrassment, personal symbols are welcome. Also, students may draw embarrassing moments of others, since they may not admit to their own experiences. The point is that what is really embarrassing may never be drawn, and what is really drawn is not really embarrassing. Encourage students to draw a comical scene, thus avoiding the embarrassment. People need not be drawn.

Evaluation: Based on the unique quality of the embarrassing experience in relation to the manner in which it is expressed and arranged. Also based on the usual elements of composition.

LESSON 201   Birth and Death   **Beginning/Intermediate/Advanced**

Purpose: To express birth and death in a single picture and within a certain time frame.

Materials: Pencils, white paper (9" x 12").

Procedure: Have students draw within a single picture the birth and death situation. It can be set within the family unit, a work unit, a hospital environment, or accidental circumstances. It can also relate to animal or plant life. Don't suggest the possibilities. Let the students ask the questions. If time allows, encourage shading, contrast, textures, and details.

98

Evaluation: Based on the convincing manner in which the situation is expressed and in the welding of the two extremes. The emotional expression of the situation is vital to proper evaluation. The setting or locale of the experiences is also important.

LESSON 202 The Funeral   Beginning/Intermediate/Advanced

Purpose: To express a highly emotional theme within a limited time frame.

Materials: Pencils, white paper (9" x 12").

Procedure: Have students consider the personal anguish of the loss of a loved one. Since this activity is to be executed in a brief period of time (one hour), it may be wise to suggest this assignment a day in advance. Encourage a close-up view of the grieving participants. Facial expressions and distorted bodies should emphasize the gravity of the situation. The location of the funeral is also important: funeral parlor, church, cemetery.

Evaluation: Based on the emotional content, distortion, location and social and economic setting of the funeral.

LESSON 203 The Wedding   Beginning/Intermediate/Advanced

Purpose: To express a joyful experience within a limited time frame.

Materials: Pencils, white paper (9" x 12").

Procedure: Have students express in a single picture the joy of a wedding and all of its ramifications. Scenes can depict any of the many facets of the wedding experience: preparations, rehearsal, church ceremony, reception. Encourage the students to express the joy of the union and the happiness that prevails among those attending.

Evaluation: Based on emotional content, subjective or objective portrayal, complexity or simplicity of the composition, and the unity of the whole.

LESSON 204 Graduation   Beginning/Intermediate/Advanced

Purpose: To express the significance of high school graduation.

Materials: Pencils, white paper (9" x 12").

Procedure: Have students avoid the usual processional lines, and focus instead on a close-up view of particular participants, reflecting the excitement of a four-year culmination of studies. The background of the drawing may consist of the attending crowd. Students should concentrate on facial expressions.

Evaluation: Based on the excitement generated by the drawing, this would depend partly on the compositional approach.

LESSON 205   Job Interview   Beginning/Intermediate/Advanced

Purpose: To illustrate a communication between two people in a single expression.

Materials: Pencils, white paper (9″ x 12″).

Procedure: Because the interview involves at least two participants, have students draw the communication, or lack of it, between two people. Students should realize that the theme can be approached in various ways: waiting in the outer office, the interview itself, the aftermath. Encourage unusual angles of composition. Facial expressions are important.

Evaluation: Based on the convincing manner in which the applicant reflects success or failure. Also based on usual compositional elements.

LESSON 206   Talent Show   Beginning/Intermediate/Advanced.

Purpose: To express in a single picture the effects a talent show has upon its audience.

Materials: Pencils, white paper (9″ x 12″).

Procedure: Have students draw the reaction of the audience to a group of talent-show performers. Include in the drawing a segment of the talent performance through some form of identification.

Evaluation: Based on the various reactions of the audience as well as the unusual manner in which the performers are identified. Composition is always important.

LESSON 207   Dining Out   Beginning/Intermediate/Advanced

Purpose: To express the various ways of dining out in a single picture within a given time frame.

Materials: Pencils, white paper (9″ x 12″).

Procedure: Have students first consider the many ways of dining out: husband-wife, mother-father, father-son, mother-daughter, family of four, family of fourteen (what about the dog?), young folks, old folks, in a cafe, at a drive-in, picnic, candlelight. Possibilities seem endless. Have them draw, remembering to show facial expressions.

Evaluation: Based on the emotional content and arrangement of the eating session.

LESSON 208   A Restless Night   **Beginning/Intermediate/Advanced**

Purpose: To express in a suggestive manner a rather difficult topic.

Materials: Pencils, white paper (9″ x 12″).

Procedure: Have students draw their interpretations of a restless night. This is not easy. Suggest alternatives to a restful night. Lack of sleep is not always a cause. The theme can also relate to the morning-after appearance. Have students focus on a central person through distortion and exaggeration. A possibility would be to show the condition of the bedroom minus the human element.

Evaluation: Based on the vivid interpretation of the theme.

LESSON 209   Popcorn Factory   **Beginning/Intermediate/Advanced**

Purpose: To test the imagination with an unusual topic.

Materials: Pencils, white paper (9″ x 12″).

Procedure: Have students draw their interpretations of a popcorn factory. No holds barred. Students should imagine the most fantastic ideas relating to the making of popcorn. It can be a small- or large-scale production.

Evaluation: Based on unusual interpretation and any unusual form of composition.

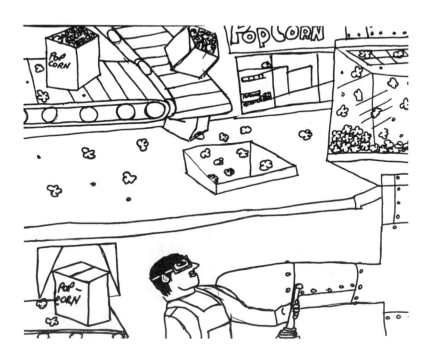

The Popcorn Factory

LESSON 210   Drive-in Theater   **Beginning/Intermediate/Advanced**

Purpose: To explore the various events that occur at a drive-in theater and express related activities in detail.

Materials: Pencils, white paper (9″ x 12″).

Procedure: Have students draw in a single expression either a subjective close-up view of a single activity occurring at the drive-in theater, or a series of events from an objective viewpoint. Encourage the illustration of comical, satirical, or ironical events. Emphasize unusual or uncommon arrangement.

Evaluation: Based on personal interpretation and unusual composition and details making for a convincing portrayal.

LESSON 211   Waiting at the Airport   **Beginning/Intermediate/Advanced**

Purpose: To express the many facets of anxiety and anticipation involved in waiting for distant arrivals.

Materials: Pencils, white paper (9″ x 12″).

Procedure: Have students reflect on their moments of anxiety, loneliness, disgust, boredom, anticipation, or excitement in waiting for the arrival of friends or relatives. Personal experiences will help them to draw reactions to the waiting period. If the plane is late in arrival due to stormy weather, strikes, accidents, or any unpredicted events, have students draw a close-up view of the facial expressions caused by such events. Loneliness may be shown by a single person waiting in an otherwise empty waiting room.

Evaluation: Based on emotional content and the close-up or unusual view depicting the content.

LESSON 212   Senior Prom   **Beginning/Intermediate/Advanced**

Purpose: To draw in a single picture the excitement or sorrow of an important school event.

Materials: Pencils, white paper (9″ x 12″).

Procedure: Have students draw their anticipation or reaction to the senior prom. This is an excellent opportunity to make a personal commentary about the validity of or need for such an event. It can be expressed as a flop or a great success.

Evaluation: Based on the subjective rather than the objective presentation of the idea.

LESSON 213 **Cafeteria Line**   **Beginning/Intermediate/Advanced**

Purpose: To express in the form of a drawing facial expressions relating to the choice of foods.

Materials: Pencils, white paper (9" x 12").

Procedure: Have students draw in a single picture the facial expressions of people in a cafeteria line. The gestures could be an interchange between the server and the diner, the servers behind the cafeteria line, or the eaters waiting in line. Avoiding all human contact, much can be made of the serving trays to express social commentary.

Evaluation: Based on the social commentary or emotional content shown in the faces of the participants.

LESSON 214 **The Clown**   **Beginning/Intermediate/Advanced**

Purpose: To attempt to draw in a single picture the many sides of a clown.

Materials: Pencils, white paper (9" x 12").

Procedure: Have students draw on white paper the various emotional changes in a clown. Leave the method of portrayal up to the students. A difficult approach would be to register dual emotions within a single portrayal of the clown.

Evaluation: Based on the unique way various emotional states are expressed.

LESSON 215 **Supermarket Check-out**   **Beginning/Intermediate/Advanced**

Purpose: To draw within a limited time frame a reaction to a phase of the check-out service at a major supermarket.

Materials: Pencils, white paper (9" x 12").

Procedure: Have students consider various times to depict the check-out service at a large supermarket. Consider early morning, noon, suppertime, late night. Then draw. Indicate that the time determines the number of customers checking out. What happens when long lines await the cashier? What happens when there are no shoppers? Encourage an approach using unusual angles.

Evaluation: Based on imaginative use of composition and social commentary, as well as detailed drawing.

LESSON 216   **The Bread Line**   **Beginning/Intermediate/Advanced**

Purpose: To record on paper the emotional tension present in the Great Depression bread lines.

Materials: Pencils, white paper (9″ x 12″).

Procedure: Have students visualize the reoccurrence of the "bread line." Since any familiarity with the topic would be secondhand, the students must, if possible, transplant the Depression theme to the present. How would students react? Have them draw a present-day bread line.

Evaluation: Based on the authenticity and emotional content of the drawing, and on the focal point of attention.

LESSON 217   **Day at the Circus**   **Beginning/Intermediate/Advanced**

Purpose: To express the various activities witnessed at the circus.

Materials: Pencils, white paper (9″ x 12″).

Procedure: Have students concentrate on a single act of the circus, drawing that as the focal point. The background should be reserved for the many other activities taking place. It is important to detail the central act and diminish in detail those performers drawn in the background.

Evaluation: Based on the detailed expression of the central activity and the background as it serves the whole.

LESSON 218   **Haunted House**   **Beginning/Intermediate/Advanced**

Purpose: To express in detail the various elements of a haunted house.

Materials: Pencils, white paper (9″ x 12″).

Procedure: Have students draw in a single picture a close-up view of various adjoining rooms within a haunted house, employing devices that lend themselves to the theme.

Evaluation: Based on the eerie feeling of the picture and the possibility of its use for future painting.

LESSON 219   Third World War   Intermediate/Advanced

Purpose: To express the possibility of a third World War and its implications for the future of young people.

Materials: Pencils, white paper (9" x 12").

Procedure: Have students reflect on the future should a third World War occur. Have them draw their interpretation of their country's reaction to it, and the resulting activities. Let this be a truly personal approach.

Evaluation: Based on the honesty of the statements and the convincing manner in which they are expressed.

LESSON 220   Working in a Bakery   Beginning/Intermediate/Advanced

Purpose: To incorporate into a single picture the various jobs of the baking business.

Materials: Pencils, white paper (9" x 12").

Procedure: Have students draw within a limited time span the series of activities involved in the making of a loaf of bread. The students may consider a single activity at close range. Finished products within the display cases may be considered.

Evaluation: Based on the inventive approach to the theme as well as the arrangement of the ideas.

LESSON 221   The Fire Alarm   Beginning/Intermediate/Advanced

Purpose: To express the excitement generated by the sound of the fire alarm.

Materials: Pencils, white paper (9" x 12").

Procedure: This is an exciting idea with far-reaching possibilities of expression. Have students consider the various interpretations of the fire alarm, including the location and the after-effects of the alarm being sounded. Can you imagine a fire alarm sounding in a packed arena of football fans, or a rock concert suddenly being dispersed, or an alarm ringing during a school cafeteria lunch hour? What about a false alarm? Have students draw a single site after the alarm has been sounded, showing the effects.

Evaluation: Based on the originality of circumstances and the effects shown.

LESSON 222   Political Campaign   Beginning/Intermediate/Advanced

Purpose: To express reactions to current political campaigning.

Materials: Pencils, white paper (9″ x 12″).

Procedure: Have students draw in a single picture the opposing factions of the two major political parties. Activities are numerous: speeches, dinners, voting, fund raising. Encourage illustration of speeches so that a crowd can be used to express emotional reactions to the politicians. Emphasize the interchange between speaker and audience.

Evaluation: Based on intensity of expression and compositional angle.

LESSON 223   Loneliness   Beginning/Intermediate/Advanced

Purpose: To express realism through the use of an abstract word.

Materials: Pencils, white paper (9″ x 12″).

Procedure: The word itself can be described with various symbols. Have students express the feeling of loneliness by drawing a visual example of loneliness. Any further instructions may spoil it.

For yourself, consider loneliness in a crowd, or fulfillment or companionship while apparently alone. The word **loneliness** has many meanings. Allow students to draw their own.

Evaluation: Based on the arrangement of the symbols of loneliness, and the emotional content.

LESSON 224   Happiness   Beginning/Intermediate/Advanced

Purpose: To express in visual terms the abstract word **happiness.**

Materials: Pencils, white paper (9″ x 12″).

Procedure: Have students consider general happy events. Then have them draw individual events reflecting this happiness. Students should consider the cause of the happiness, which may be symbolized by a single item such as an engagement ring, high school diploma, or driver's license. Draw a close-up view of the recipient and the symbol of happiness.

Evaluation: Based on the provocative nature of the symbolism and the arrangement of the idea.

LESSON 225   **Love**   **Beginning/Intermediate/Advanced**

Purpose: To express in symbols the abstract word **love.**

Materials: Pencils, white paper (9" x 12").

Procedure: Have students draw within a brief period of time their interpretation of love. Students should use symbolic objects in a common-sense arrangement of receding and advancing planes. Love denotes an extreme fondness which could incorporate love between human beings, love of animals, love of work, love of a place.

Evaluation: Based on the interpretation, emotional content, and arrangement.

LESSON 226   **Hate**   **Beginning/Intermediate/Advanced**

Purpose: To express in a subjective or objective portrayal the abstract word **hate.**

Materials: Pencils, white paper (9" x 12").

Procedure: Have students draw in a common-sense arrangement their interpretations of hate. It should be reflected in an emotional reaction to an idea or a physical act. Students should think thoroughly about their interpretations before drawing them. Remember, the interpretation in a natural setting is foremost. Any additional relative items are fine if they enhance the expression.

Evaluation: Based on the depth of interpretation and understanding of the word, and its subsequent expression.

LESSON 227   **Limitation Using a Holiday Theme**   **Beginning/Intermediate/Advanced**

Purpose: To limit the number of objects drawn in a single expression, adding only those objects relating to holiday themes.

Materials: Pencils, white paper (9" x 12").

Procedure: Have students draw the following in a single picture: three houses, four trees, one fence. Draw no more, no less. After drawing is complete, add objects involving a particular holiday; for example, Halloween would invite the addition of a cat on the fence, an owl in a tree, pumpkins by the houses, or witches in the sky.

Evaluation: Based on the use of the limitation process and the appropriateness of the seasonal objects.

LESSON 228   Band Practice   **Beginning/Intermediate/Advanced**

Purpose: To express in a single picture and within a limited time frame segments of a band rehearsal.

Materials: Pencils, white paper (9" x 12").

Procedure: Have students draw one of several activities involved in band rehearsal: setting up, the actual rehearsal, putting away, audience, close-up of a single instrumentalist or the director. Major concerns for students should be the arrangement of band members, or the close-up view of the director or an individual performer.

Evaluation: Based on compositional unity of all segments of the band and/or the communication between director and individual performer.

LESSON 229   The Whistle Blew   **Beginning/Intermediate/Advanced**

Purpose: To express a single idea, or various possibilities within a single picture, interpreting situations reflecting a particular theme.

Materials: Pencils, white paper (9" x 12").

Procedure: Have students draw their interpretations of a situation occurring under various different circumstances. They should draw an idea anticipating the action following a blown whistle, such as the traffic cop's whistle, the referee's whistle, the factory whistle, the tea kettle whistle, and whistles of unknown origins. Each circumstance causes different reactions. Have students draw a single event.

Evaluation: Based on action and emotional content.

LESSON 230   Series of Blown Whistles   **Intermediate/Advanced**

Purpose: To draw in a single picture and within a limited time frame three events occurring simultaneously.

Materials: Pencils, white paper (9" x 12").

Procedure: Draw in a single picture at least three different events caused by the blowing of a whistle. The picture must show a continuity of events so that three separate events take place simultaneously, not necessarily one causing the other. The picture may be a close-up, or at a distance, or a combination of both.

Evaluation: Based on the choice of events and their organization.

LESSON 231   Taxi, Please!   **Beginning/Intermediate/Advanced**

Purpose: To express a situation hinging on various emotional circumstances.

Materials: Pencils, white paper (9″ x 12″).

Procedure: Have students draw a situation reflecting the need for a taxicab. Consideration should be given to circumstances causing the need, such as inclement weather, work tardiness, emergency, or catching a train or plane. This calls for student reaction. Encourage students to consider the unusual, the angle of viewing, and close-up contact with the parties involved.

Evaluation: Based on the circumstances shown and the angle or arrangement of the idea.

LESSON 232   A Day at the Races   **Beginning/Intermediate/Advanced**

Purpose: To express quickly an idea related to a day at the races.

Materials: Pencils, white paper (9″ x 12″).

Procedure: Have students draw in a single picture their notions of the theme. (Consider the different types of races, such as dog racing, horse racing, car racing, boat racing, and various forms of human racing. These need not be mentioned to the students.)

Evaluation: Based on the choice of race and the imaginative manner in which it is represented, composed, and arranged.

LESSON 233   The Picket Line   **Beginning/Intermediate/Advanced**

Purpose: To express reactions to a common event in American life.

Materials: Pencils, white paper (9″ x 12″).

Procedure: Have students draw in a single picture and within a limited time frame their notions of the picket line. Display reasons for or against the cause of those picketing. Consider the unusual. The picture should be more than a group of posters. It should make a significant contribution toward a future painting.

Evaluation: Based on the general criteria of composition, idea, technique, and emotional content.

LESSON 234   The Corner Newsstand   Beginning/Intermediate/Advanced

Purpose: To recall and draw the idea of the corner newsstand, or its counterpart today.

Materials: Pencils, white paper (9" x 12").

Procedure: Have students draw the equivalent of the corner newsstand. Explain the corner newsstand as it existed years ago. Suggest that they show the panorama of the variety of titles, or a close-up view of a few selections. What type of person sells, and who buys? Background can also be important.

Evaluation: Based on unusual approach and emotional content.

LESSON 235   The Post Office at Christmas Time Beginning/Intermediate/Advanced

Purpose: To express in a single picture and within a limited time span the events of a post-office rush time.

Materials: Pencils, white paper (9" x 12").

Procedure: Have students draw in a single picture the situation at the local post office during the Christmas rush. Students are free to express any segment of the post office operation.

Evaluation: Based on the originality of the ideas and their arrangement.

LESSON 236   City Dump   Beginning/Intermediate/Advanced

Purpose: To use an "unglamorous" theme as a means of artistic expression.

Materials: Pencils, white paper (9" x 12").

Procedure: This topic is wide open. Have students draw in a single picture their interpretations of the city dump. Its location is important to social commentary. Encourage students to use theme in an unusual manner. Be alert to compositional angles.

Evaluation: Based on the unusual use of the theme, and the strength of the composition in terms of the idea.

LESSON 237   **The Rescue**   Beginning/Intermediate/Advanced

Purpose: To draw an interpretation of a single word within a given period of time.

Materials: Pencils, white paper (9″ x 12″).

Procedure: Have students draw their interpretations of the word **rescue.** The word suggests various activities, such as rescuing victims from drowning, fire, accidents, or illness. These, in turn, suggest several other events. Encourage a close-up view of unusual events showing both the victim and rescuer. Work to show emotional reactions of both parties.

Evaluation: Based on compositional unity and emotional content.

LESSON 238   **The Fire Plug**   Beginning/Intermediate/Advanced

Purpose: To express in visual terms a single item and an event related to it.

Materials: Pencils, white paper (9″ x 12″).

Procedure: Have students draw their interpretations of an event stemming from the presence or use of the fire plug. A close-up view is suggested, but objective portrayal could lead to interesting events.

Evaluation: Based on the unusual use of the fire plug, and compositional unity.

LESSON 239   **The Flood**   Beginning/Intermediate/Advanced

Purpose: To translate a tragic event into artistic expression.

Materials: Pencils, white paper (9″ x 12″).

Procedure: Have students draw their interpretations of a flood. Again, the word suggests various phenomena, such as flooded basements, streets, roads and highways, towns, and farmlands. Encourage the unusual.

Evaluation: Based on the personal approach and the effects shown, and the convincing manner of expression.

LESSON 240   The Park Bench   **Beginning/Intermediate/Advanced**

Purpose: To consider a single item of various uses as a means of artistic expression.

Materials: Pencils, white paper (9″ x 12″).

Procedure: A provocative theme encourages provocative ideas. Have students consider the full gamut of possibilities of the park bench. The type of occupant is important. Also consider it without occupants. The location of the park bench may suggest a social commentary. View of the bench is important as well as a close-up view of its occupants.

Evaluation: Based on the uses shown, and the social commentary.

LESSON 241   The Pet Show   **Beginning/Intermediate/Advanced**

Purpose: To record the relationship of the animal and human breed.

Materials: Pencils, white paper (9″ x 12″).

Procedure: A pet show is an ego trip, not for the pets, but for the owners. This is a good chance for the animal artist to show his or her talents by lining up the various breeds and types of pets. Perhaps more important is the relationship between pet and owner. Have students draw personal interpretations of the pet show. Close-up views would be particularly appropriate.

Evaluation: Based on the pet personalities shown, and on the portrayal of the pet-and-owner relationship.

LESSON 242   Sunday Picnic   **Beginning/Intermediate/Advanced**

Purpose: To express in a limited period of time a personal interpretation of a single theme.

Materials: Pencils, white paper (9″ x 12″).

Procedure: A traditional Sunday affair could become an exciting experience. Have students draw the theme. Give them no other hints. Let them interpret it in the broadest sense.

Evaluation: Based on unusual approach to the idea, and its arrangement.

LESSON 243   Trash Pickup   Beginning/Intermediate/Advanced

Purpose: To compose a nonattractive event into an artistic expression.

Materials: Pencils, white paper (9" x 12").

Procedure: Have students record a trash theme on paper, showing a single aspect or combining several aspects into a single expression. The ugliness of trash can be converted into an unusual or attractive composition. Consider the social and economic implications of the trash pileup. Focusing on a particular object in the trash will help to identify the past owners.

Evaluation: Based on the imaginative concept of the composition as well as the use of contrast, texture, and details.

LESSON 244   The Car Wash   Beginning/Intermediate/Advanced

Purpose: To record in a single picture the activity of the car wash.

Materials: Pencils, white paper (9" x 12").

Procedure: Have students draw within a limited time frame an unusual view of the car line-up. A rear view, an overall view, a front view, an inside-the-car view are all possibilities. If people are to be drawn, have students reflect on the machine operators. There are other types of car washes. Perhaps the students will think of them.

Evaluation: Based on the original use of the theme and the manner in which it is composed.

LESSON 245   The Dog Fight   Beginning/Intermediate/Advanced

Purpose: To record in a brief period of time in the form of a drawing an unusual theme.

Materials: Pencils, white paper (9" x 12").

Procedure: Have students draw a dog fight in a single picture. Consider the two words, **dog** and **fight.** Students might also consider the possibility of a second party, a human being or another type of animal. A dog fight does not necessarily mean a fight among dogs.

Evaluation: Based on the originality of interpretation, and emotional content displayed.

CHAPTER VI PRACTICAL EXERCISES IN ART APPRECIATION

LESSON 246   Naturalism: Single Object   **Intermediate/Advanced**

Purpose: To record as accurately as possible the visual appearance of a single aspect of
nature.

Materials: Pencils, white drawing paper, tempera paint, brushes, paint trays, water cups.

Procedure: Have students select a natural object, draw it on white paper, and paint it according to its exact appearance. This rendering should include texture, contrast, details, and three-dimensional qualities.

Evaluation: Based solely on the duplication of the original object.

Displaced Child

LESSON 247 **Naturalism: Natural Setting** Intermediate/Advanced

Purpose: To record exactly an outside scene minus all objects.

Materials: Pencils, white drawing paper, tempera paint, paint trays, water cups, brushes.

Procedure: Have students draw on white paper an outdoor scene that includes only the sky and land, or sky, land, and water. Then have them first paint the sky as it actually appears to the viewer. Stormy, snowy, rainy, and sunny skies will differ in appearance. Colors will vary in each sky. For example, if the sky is sunny, paint the upper half bright blue. Blend white into the blue so the sky appears bright blue at the top, fading to very light blue at the horizon. This requires wet paint on the surface of the paper at all times. Similarly, the ground, if grass, should go from dark green to light or bright green as it leads from the horizon line to the bottom of the paper. Texture and details such as blades of grass should then be applied one by one.

Evaluation: Based completely on the accurate appearance of the scene, including recessive and advancing qualities, textures, and details.

LESSON 248 **Naturalism: Presence of Objects in Setting** Intermediate/Advanced

Purpose: To record a natural setting, complete with background and accompanying objects.

Materials: Pencils, white drawing paper, tempera paint, paint trays, water cups, brushes.

Procedure: Have students draw on white paper an outdoor scene, showing a natural setting with accompanying aspects. Have them first paint the recessive and advancing qualities of the sky and the ground. Allow to dry. Then have the single aspect of nature painted to tie in with the background. The result should be an accurate duplication of the visual scene.

Evaluation: Based completely on the accurate appearance of the scene, including recessive and advancing qualities, textures, and details.

LESSON 249 **Realism: Distortion of Technique** Intermediate/Advanced

Purpose: To present realism through distortion of color application technique.

Materials: Pencils, white drawing paper, tempera paint, paint trays, water cups, brushes.

Procedure: Have students draw an outdoor scene realistically on white paper. Apply color in such a way as to change the original atmosphere of the scene. A sunny day will appear stormy, if the paint is applied to the sky area in a dramatic mixture of colors representing the emotional atmosphere. The change of sky will automatically force a change in other areas of the painting.

Evaluation: Based on the emotional appearance of the stormy scene.

LESSON 250 **Realism: Distortion of Objects** Intermediate/Advanced

Purpose: To express realism in a painting through the distortion of objects.

Materials: Pencils, white drawing paper, tempera paint, paint trays, water cups, brushes.

Procedure: Have students draw on white paper a group of figures engaged in some form of activity. The drawing must be distorted or exaggerated beyond the natural appearance in order to make the activity more dramatic. For example, figures may be elongated to represent a tragic or sorrowful event. Have students consider facial distortion as a means of promoting expression of emotion. Drawings are then painted.

Evaluation: Based on the distortion of the figures in relation to the activity.

LESSON 251 **Realism: Distortion of Color** Intermediate/Advanced

Purpose: To express realism in a painting through the use of color distortion.

Materials: Pencils, white drawing paper, tempera paint, paint trays, water cups, brushes.

Procedure: Have students draw an outside scene on white paper. Apply tempera paint to those areas in which an emotional change is needed. For example, red would promote the feeling of warmth. Cool colors may suggest sorrow or calm. The colors should appear realistic in terms of human emotion rather than natural in terms of visual appearance. Let the colors charge the painting with emotion.

Evaluation: Based on the use of color in causing a change in emotional reaction. A good composition is presumed to be present before the painting begins.

LESSON 252 **Cool Impressionism** Beginning/Intermediate/Advanced

Purpose: To understand and appreciate Impressionism through the medium of painting.

Materials: Pencils, white drawing paper, tempera paint, paint trays, brushes, water cups.

Procedure: Have students draw an outdoor scene on white paper. Using the cool colors of blue, purple, green, and grey, apply dots of color with the point of the brush. The dots should be placed in a given area, such as a grassy area with dots of green and white. The dots should be side by side, barely touching each other, so that from a distance they appear to blend. To darken the grass area, add dots of blue. A sky area should be dots of blue and purple, lightened where necessary with dots of white. Be sure that there is a consistency of dot size. Be careful of blotches of color. Contrast can be strengthened by using darker colors in an area where two sections join.

Evaluation: Based on the accurate placement of color dots, forming a single color.

LESSON 253   **Warm Impressionism**   **Beginning/Intermediate/Advanced**

Purpose: To understand and appreciate Impressionism through the medium of painting.

Materials: Pencils, white drawing paper, tempera paint, paint trays, water cups, brushes.

Procedure: Have students draw a still life of flowers on white paper. Using the warm colors of yellow, orange, and red, apply side-by-side dots of color with the point of the brush. If a yellow-orange is to be mixed, more dots of yellow than orange should be applied. Contrasts again are formed by applying darker colors. White dots may be added to lighten an area, brown dots to darken. The painting is not complete until the entire surface of the white paper is dotted with color.

Evaluation: Based on the accurate placement of color dots to form single colors in a complete painting.

LESSON 254   **Surrealism: Real Objects in Unreal Setting**   **Intermediate/Advanced**

Purpose: To execute a surrealistic painting through an unusual background surface.

Materials: Pencils, white drawing paper, tempera paint, paint trays, water cups, brushes.

Procedure: Have students first draw, then paint a realistic portrayal of a landscape. Redraw the picture on a second piece of white paper. In the second painting, retain the objects in their exact position, but reverse the background colors. The sky becomes land, and the land becomes sky. If students prefer, the sky and land can be replaced by other background materials.

Evaluation: Based on the unification and natural appearance of the objects in relation to the background.

LESSON 255   **Surrealism: Unreal Objects in Real Setting**   **Intermediate/Advanced**

Purpose: To understand surrealism through the medium of painting.

Materials: Pencils, white drawing paper, tempera paint, paint trays, water cups, brushes.

Procedure: Have students use the original realistic painting or a landscape. Redraw the picture on a second piece of white paper. Repaint the background as in the original, but change the real objects into objects of unreality. Trees may become hands springing out of the ground, blades of grass may become daggers, the sky may become a patchwork of pizza ingredients, and so forth.

Evaluation: Based on the unique interaction of the real and the unreal, and the precision of paint application. (Photo on page 118.)

Jet Pilot
(Lesson 255)

LESSON 256 Surrealism: Combination of Contrary Objects Intermediate/Advanced

Purpose: To tax the imagination by translating reality into unreality in all phases of the composition.

Materials: Pencils, white drawing paper, tempera paint, paint trays, water cups, brushes.

Procedure: Have students draw, then paint, an outdoor scene on white paper. Include houses, trees, flowers, fences, animals, sidewalks, roads. Using a second piece of paper, redraw the picture, altering all realistic objects to resemble objects that are real in themselves but appear unreal when painted into the original shapes. The background should be changed in the same manner. The completed painting involves reality, but in its combination of things appears completely surrealistic.

Evaluation: Based on the imaginative changeover of realistic objects into surreal objects. Also based on the technical application of paint and the arrangement of ideas.

LESSON 257   Optical: Cool Gradation   Intermediate/Advanced

Purpose: To introduce the principle of optical illusion through color gradations.

Materials: Pencils, rulers, white drawing paper, tempera paint, paint trays, water cups, brushes.

Procedure: Have students draw on white paper a series of parallel lines crossing the paper vertically or horizontally ½" apart. Apply white paint between the first two lines and black between the last two lines. Paint the center lane blue. Have students add a touch of blue to white, mixing until a very light blue is evident. Apply this to the second lane. Continue adding blue to white, painting lanes until a gradation of color from white to blue is achieved. From the center blue lane, add a touch of black to blue, mixing so that a color slightly darker than blue appears. Apply to the lane next to the blue lane. Continue adding black until all lanes to the right of the blue show a consistent gradation from blue to black. The final result should be a gradation from white to blue to black.

Evaluation: Based on the consistent gradation of the color.

LESSON 258   Optical Expansion   Intermediate/Advanced

Purpose: To expand the gradation process.

Materials: Pencils, rulers, white drawing paper, tempera paint, paint trays, water cups, brushes.

Procedure: Have students draw on white paper a series of parallel lines about ½" apart. Apply white paint at one end of the paper and blue at the other end. Add a touch of blue to the white and apply to the second lane. Continue process until a complete and consistent gradation appears from white to blue.

Evaluation: Based on the consistent gradation of the single primary color.

LESSON 259   Symmetrical Optical   Intermediate/Advanced

Purpose: To execute a symmetrical optical illusion in color.

Materials: Pencils, rulers, white drawing paper, tempera paint, paint trays, water cups, brushes.

120

Procedure: Have students design a symmetrical pattern on white drawing paper. Finding the center point of the paper by drawing diagonal lines from corner to corner, continue drawing lines through the center point until a suitable number of shapes are created. To be sure shapes are equal, the outside edges of the paper can be measured. After all diagonals are drawn, a rectangle is drawn near the center of the design by connecting the two lines adjacent to the center horizontal line on both sides of the vertical center line. Then connect these two vertical lines with two parallel horizontal lines, forming the rectangle. Continue this process until a suitable number of rectangles are complete. The more rectangles, the more complex the design. Add color in checkerboard fashion.

Evaluation: Based on the illusionary effects of the design.

LESSON 260   Nonsymmetrical Optical   Beginning/Intermediate/Advanced

Purpose: To render a nonsymmetrical optical illusion in color.

Materials: Pencils, white drawing paper, rulers, tempera paint, paint trays, water cups, brushes.

Procedure: Have students draw on white paper a series of diagonal lines crisscrossing each other from one edge of the paper to the other, varying the shapes as they are formed. Apply green and red tempera paint, alternating the colors in checkerboard fashion. Changes will be made as the design progresses.

Evaluation: Based on the illusionary effects of the design.

LESSON 261   Semi-Optical   Beginning/Intermediate/Advanced

Purpose: To transform realism into an optical illusion.

Materials: Pencils, white drawing paper, tempera paint, paint trays, water cups, brushes.

Procedure: Have students draw a realistic picture on white paper. In each area of the picture have lines drawn parallel to each other so that each section of lines opposes adjoining lines. For example, if the lines in a sky area are drawn horizontally, then the clouds should have vertical lines. Each section of the picture should have such lines. Colors are then selected and applied to each area, two colors for each section. Blue and white, alternating, will be painted horizontally into the sky. Grey and black may be used for the cloud section, but vertically. The entire picture is painted in sections of two alternating colors. Students must be alert to contrasting combinations. All elements of composition should be considered, such as recession and advancement of colors.

Evaluation: Based on the optical effects of the painting and retention of the original idea.

LESSON 262   Three Optical Focal Points   Intermediate/Advanced

Purpose: To expand the optical illusion into variants of three primary colors.

Materials: Pencils, rulers, white drawing paper, tempera paint, paint trays, water cups, brushes.

Procedure: Have students select three focal points on the surface of the paper. Then draw several lines through each point, extending lines to the edges of the paper. After all lines are drawn, select the three primary colors. Paint one section with blue-to-white gradations. Do the same with red-to-white and yellow-to-white. Where the colors overlap, apply secondary colors. The final optical painting should include variations of blue, yellow, red, orange, green, and purple. Since this is an extensive assignment, small paper is advised.

Evaluation: Based on the illusionary effects and complexity of the design.

LESSON 263 Optical Cube   Beginning/Intermediate/Advanced

Purpose: To express an optical illusion in three-dimensional design.

Materials: Pencils, rulers, white drawing paper, 3-D container, tempera paint, paint trays, water cups, brushes, glue.

Procedure: Have students select a 3-D shape, such as a toothpaste or medicine box. Have box painted with a dark color. After paint is dry, draw parallel lines on one side and extend them to all four sides of the box. Using the background color and a second color, alternate the lanes so that a repeat pattern is established on one side of the box. Use the same colors on the second side of the box, but reverse their positions. Continue the process until all four sides of the box are painted. Sides one and three should match, and sides two and four should match.

Evaluation: Based on the optical three-dimensional effects.

LESSON 264 Free-Form Abstract   Beginning/Intermediate/Advanced

Purpose: To demonstrate a basic knowledge of color through the use of abstract design.

Materials: Pencils, white drawing paper, tempera paint, paint trays, water cups, brushes.

Procedure: Have students draw a free-flowing scribble on white paper, overlapping the lines so that shapes are formed. Have students consider variety of shapes and sizes. Students should label all shapes with colors to be used, considering the mixture of primary colors. Two overlapping shapes of red and yellow will create a third color (orange) in the overlap area. Likewise, overlapping of blue and yellow causes green, and purple stems from the overlap of red and blue. The insertion of a secondary color between two primary colors is necessary to sustain the original design.

Evaluation: Based on the fluidity and completeness of design as well as the variety of sizes, shapes, and colors.

LESSON 265 Geometric Abstract   Beginning/Intermediate/Advanced

Purpose: To execute an abstract design using various overlapping geometric shapes.

Materials: Pencils, rulers, white drawing paper, tempera paint, paint trays, water cups, brushes.

Procedure: Have students draw, with rulers, geometric shapes in an overlapping style. Label all shapes with colors to be used, considering secondary colors created by overlapping primary colors. No primary colors should be adjacent to each other. For example, purple should be flanked by blue and red, orange by red and yellow, green by blue and yellow. If neutral shapes exist in which no colors overlap, then grey is painted in that area. This maintains the original design.

Evaluation: Based on the precise and accurate blending of overlapping colors.

LESSONS 266 Semi-Abstract   Beginning/Intermediate/Advanced

Purpose: To transform a realistic idea into an abstract painting.

Materials: Pencils, white drawing paper, tempera paint, paint trays, water cups, brushes.

Procedure: Have students draw, on white paper, a visual stimulus such as a still life, landscape, or figures. Draw objects in overlapping fashion. Extend background lines through objects in the foreground. For example, in a landscape with clouds drawn behind treetops, the lines of the clouds will be drawn over the lines of the treetops so that both the clouds and the treetops can be viewed completely and simultaneously. In painting the picture, the treetops would be painted black, the clouds white, and those sections of the treetops overlapping the clouds would be painted grey (the combination of the colors black and white). This is necessary to sustain the complete painting. It is called interpenetration, the theory of bringing forward that which is back and pushing back that which is forward.

Evaluation: Based on the transformation of realism to semi-abstraction. (Photo on page 124.)

124

Speed Limit

LESSON 267 Flat Pattern Abstract   **Beginning/Intermediate/Advanced**

Purpose: To introduce a simple form of abstract design.

Materials: Pencils, white drawing paper, tempera paint, paint trays, water cups, brushes.

Procedure: Have students draw a controlled doodle on white paper, crisscrossing lines so that various shapes are formed. Then have shapes painted, each in a different color. Balance of color, size, and shape is of major concern. The result should be an appealing balance of color throughout the composition.

Evaluation: Based solely on the balance of color according to variety of shapes and sizes.

Record Player and Sports

LESSON 268 Semi-Cubism   **Beginning/Intermediate/Advanced**

Purpose: To transform a realistic picture into a semi-cubist one.

Materials: Pencils, white drawing paper, tempera paint, paint trays, water cups, brushes.

Procedure: Have students draw a realistic picture, preferably a scene of buildings. Redraw on white paper, transforming each shape into a cube. Paint each shape so that the two visible sides are two tones of the same color and the top, if visible, is a third tone. Remember, all shapes should be transformed into cubes, even the sky.

Evaluation: Based on the cube appearance and the unity of color.

Buildings

LESSON 269   Cubism   Beginning/Intermediate/Advanced

Purpose: To execute a nonobjective painting composed entirely of cubes.

Materials: Pencils, white drawing paper, tempera paint, paint trays, water cups, brushes.

Procedure: Have students draw an allover pattern of cubes on white paper. Select colors. Apply three tones of a single color to each cube. In painting, the left side of each cube should be the dark tone, the top side the light tone, and the right side the medium tone. Any color can be used, as well as black and white.

Evaluation: Based on the general neatness of the painting and the overall unity of contrasts.

LESSON 270   Pop Art: Singular   Beginning/Intermediate/Advanced

Purpose: To express in contemporary fashion a commercial product popular among the students.

Materials: Pencils, white drawing paper, tempera paint, paint trays, water cups, brushes.

Procedure: Have students draw on white paper an enlargement of a commercial product, such as chewing gum, soda, or toothpaste. Any commodity that is thrust at the public via television, radio, and newspaper is a worthy victim. Have the enlarged product painted in an exact portrayal of the original.

Evaluation: Based on accurate drawing, painting, and enlargement of the original product.

LESSON 271   Pop Art: Allover Pattern   Beginning/Intermediate/Advanced

Purpose: To execute a duplicate of a commercial product in repeat pattern.

Materials: Pencils, white drawing paper, tempera paint, paint trays, water cups, brushes.

Procedure: Have students draw a reproduction of a single commercial product, repeating to create an allover pattern. To facilitate the drawing, a copy of the product can be cut from tagboard and traced onto white paper into the allover pattern. (The most obvious example is Andy Warhol's painting, "Campbell's Soup Cans.") The students should consider only commercial products appropriate to their concerns. Have students complete their allover patterns in tempera.

Evaluation: Based on the choice of product, the effect of the repeat pattern, and neatness.

LESSON 272 Abstract Expressionism   **Intermediate/Advanced**

Purpose: To paint a direct emotional reaction to an idea.

Materials: Pencils, white drawing paper, tempera paint, paint trays, water cups, brushes.

Procedure: Have students select a tragic or joyful event, such as death, birth, rebirth, or accident. Students should build up an emotional fervor toward the idea, then paint directly onto paper their emotional reactions to it. There is no preparation beforehand except for forming mental images of what is to be painted. Colors and techniques are applied spontaneously. The composition should emerge instinctively as the painting progresses.

Evaluation: Based on the emotional content stemming from intuitive responses to the idea.

Easter

LESSON 273   **Expressionism from Visual Stimuli**   **Intermediate/Advanced**

Purpose: To paint intuitively from visual stimuli.

Materials: Pencils, white drawing paper, tempera paint, paint trays, water cups, brushes.

Procedure: Have students paint a still life on large white drawing paper. Using a brush, they should lay out the entire composition before painting the objects. Students should feel free to change the stimulus, either in color or shape, to their individual temperaments. The painting should be completed within an hour. If an error is made, it is sponged out, painted over, or used to suggest a different direction.

Evaluation: Based on the convincing appearance of the painting and the intuitive response to the visual stimulus.

LESSON 274   **Pop-Op Painting**   **Intermediate/Advanced**

Purpose: To incorporate two schools of painting into a single expression.

Materials: Pencils, white drawing paper, tempera paint, paint trays, water cups, brushes.

Procedure: Have students draw a commercial product in Pop fashion as accurately as possible on white drawing paper. Then devise an allover optical pattern to be drawn in the space surrounding the object. Be sure the optical pattern does not overpower the Pop segment of the painting. Paint optical background in colors that create an optical illusion in unity with the Pop object.

Evaluation: Based on the compatibility of the Pop-Op combination.

Wrist Watch

LESSON 275   Op-Pop Painting   **Intermediate/Advanced**

Purpose: To incorporate two schools of painting in a single expression.

Materials: Pencils, white drawing paper, tempera paint, paint trays, water cups, brushes.

Procedure: Have students draw an allover optical pattern on white drawing paper. Paint it, except for a single area, which is painted in with a popular commercial product.

Evaluation: Based on the compatibility of the Op-Pop combination.

The Clown

CHAPTER VII AFTERTHOUGHTS ▰

LESSON 276   Pencil Montage   **Intermediate/Advanced**

Purpose: To create in multimedia an expression of visual stimuli.

Materials: Pencils, heavy white drawing paper, newspaper, glue, scissors, paper towels, paper tissues.

Procedure: Have students draw a visual stimulus (still life, landscape, posed models) on heavy white drawing paper. Then introduce various or limited types of paper. Glue paper textures onto the drawing in areas adjacent to the main ideas. Use bits of newspaper, paper towels, and tissues to enhance the drawing's appearance. The final expression should exhibit the pencil medium as foremost, with other materials subservient to it. **Do not let the background materials overpower the drawing.**

Evaluation: Based on the strength of the pencil drawing, the total composition, and the distribution of materials.

LESSON 277   Reverse Silhouette   **Beginning/Intermediate/Advanced**

Purpose: To create a nontraditional silhouette of white on black.

Materials: Pencils, white drawing paper, glue, black construction paper, scissors, X-acto knives.

Procedure: Have students draw an idea on white drawing paper. Then cut out this illustration and glue it onto black construction paper. Details can be cut from the white paper with X-acto knives, or black pieces can be cut and glued onto the white paper. The effect will be the same in either case.

Evaluation: Based on the reverse appearance of the silhouette as well as simplicity and uniformity.

LESSON 278   Stage Set Designs   **Advanced**

Purpose: To execute a series of display sets suitable for an entire theatrical production.

Materials: Pencils, drawing paper, brushes, tempera paint, water containers, scenery props, chalk or charcoal.

Procedure: Have students draw preliminary sketches for individual scenes appropriate to a play or musical. Enlarge the preliminary drawings onto wallboard, muralboard, or props with chalk or charcoal. Paint these backdrops. Remember that scenes must be viewed from a considerable distance. Thus students should keep each drawing simple, and painting should be strong in color. This can be an independent study assignment.

Evaluation: Based on effectiveness of purpose.

LESSON 279   Colored Tissue Paper Appliqué   Beginning/Intermediate/Advanced

Purpose: To create an artistic expression from accidental effects.

Materials: Colored tissue paper, brushes, glue, water, white drawing paper, pencils, scissors.

Procedure: Have students draw a preliminary sketch on white drawing paper (18″ x 24″). The drawing should be a close-up view of an idea. Avoid detailed objects. Tear or cut tissue paper to fit the ideas drawn. After diluting glue with water, place colored tissue paper over the objects drawn on the white paper. Brush over tissue paper with glue mixture so that tissue paper seems to adhere to white paper. Moistening the tissue paper causes color to be transferred from the tissue to the surface of the white drawing paper. After the drawing is completely covered with colored tissue paper, allow to dry overnight. Remove tissues, which should peel off easily. The final appearance is similar to that of a serigraph.

Evaluation: Based on total composition, idea, and professional appearance.

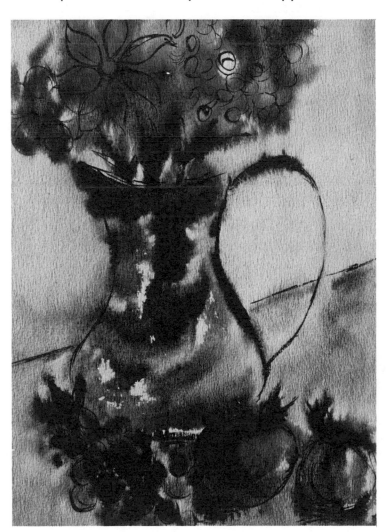

Still Life

LESSON 280   Tissue Paper Watercolor   Intermediate/Advanced

Purpose: To use the convenience of colored tissues in the watercolor technique of painting.

Materials: Colored tissue papers, white drawing paper, pencils, glue/water mixture, brushes.

Procedure: Have students draw ideas on white drawing paper. Use both the watercolor technique of painting and the application of colored tissue papers. Students will benefit from both the color bleeding of the tissues and the flexibility of watercolor brushwork. The final appearance should reflect a watercolor approach to painting.

Evaluation: Based on the flexibility and apparent freedom of the color application, plus the balance and composition of the idea.

LESSON 281   Cork Carving   Intermediate/Advanced

Purpose: To carve a three-dimensional image out of a natural piece of cork.

Materials: Natural cork, X-acto knives, sharp paring knives, long beautician's razor blades.

Procedure: Have students select a large piece of cork. Using sharp paring knives, slice away small pieces of cork until a desired shape, figure, or image emerges. If a natural idea is not suggested by the cork shape, students should consider an attractive abstract shape.

Evaluation: Based on the three-dimensional appearance of the emerging cork image.

LESSON 282   Cork Sculpture   Intermediate/Advanced

Purpose: To create a three-dimensional expression by both additive and subtractive methods.

Materials: Cork scraps, large pieces of cork, glue, X-acto knives, wood base.

Procedure: Have students select a large piece of cork as a central working piece. Add or subtract pieces of cork as the need arises. Always consider the negative and positive aspects of the sculptural form. Move upward and outward. When desired effects are achieved, have students anchor cork sculpture to wood base.

Evaluation: Based on the sculptural principles of three-dimensional viewing.

LESSON 283 Clay Sculpture   **Beginning/Intermediate/Advanced**

Purpose: To carve an abstract image from a large piece of clay.

Materials: Large piece of clay, carving tools, damp cloths, colored glazes, kiln.

Procedure: Have students work with a large piece of leathery clay. To distinguish it from carving, have students consider abstract qualities. Carve away pieces of clay as an abstract form emerges. Consider space surrounding the form as well as the form
itself. Textures can be chipped away or carved into the clay. After clay is completely dried, glazes should be added and fired at proper temperature.

Evaluation: Based on three-dimensional abstract effectiveness.

Abstract

LESSON 284   Clay Relief   **Beginning/Intermediate/Advanced**

Purpose: To execute a relief expression by pressing clay.

Materials: Large clay slab, rollers, paring knives, pressure tools, colored glazes, kiln.

Procedure: Have students work either intuitively or from preliminary sketch. Using pre-
                  pared clay, roll out a large slab. While clay is still flexible, model it in bas-relief to
                  desired effects. Pushing the clay down with various objects will form three-
                  dimensional effects, as will cutting away or digging out. After various levels of
                  modeling become evident, allow clay to dry to a leathery finish. Add linear de-
                  tails with compass point or knife. After clay is completely dry, glazes may be
                  added and fired.

Evaluation: Based on various relief modulations and general composition.

LESSON 285   Pegboard String Construction   **Intermediate/Advanced**

Purpose: To construct a free-hanging pegboard with dowels.

Materials: Large section of pegboard, several lengths of dowels, razor blades, glue, string.

Procedure: Have students select proper size and shape of pegboard. Select various lengths
                  of dowels that fit the pegboard holes. Insert dowels into holes so that they pro-
                  trude through the opposite side of the pegboard. Students will work both sides
                  of the pegboard as a complete three-dimensional project. Before dowels are in
                  place, score each end with a razor blade. Attach strings to the slits in all dowel
                  ends, gluing to secure, on both sides of the pegboard. Spacing, in addition to the
                  lengths of dowels, determines the overall design. Remember to use both sides of
                  the pegboard for a complete three-dimensional abstract design. The finished
                  product can be propped up as a stabile, or it can hang as a mobile.

Evaluation: Based on the overall three-dimensional effect.

LESSON 286   Pegboard Construction   **Beginning/Intermediate/Advanced**

Purpose: To create an abstract three-dimensional design using pegboards and dowels.

Materials: Dowels of various lengths, large piece of pegboard, glue, saw, sandpaper.

Procedure: Have students select a large piece of pegboard (24" x 48") and dowels to fit peg-
                  board holes. Saw dowels into various lengths and insert them into holes, adjust-
                  ing the lengths of each for variety. Close the ends of dowels by connecting the
                  ends of two with a third, forming a shape. Continue this process until all the
                  dowels used form a large abstract geometric shape of overlapping lines. For best

gluing results, make sure the side dowel connecting the two end dowels fits into an even horizontal plane.

Evaluation: Based solely on the variety and balance of the linear abstract total composition.

LESSON 287   Wax Carving   Beginning/Intermediate/Advanced

Purpose: To execute a carving from a three-dimensional substance.

Materials: Block of paraffin wax or candle wax (cardboard container), small paring knife.

Procedure: Have students select a block of paraffin wax, or melt down candle wax into a cardboard container suitable to the idea to be carved. Remove the container after the wax has hardened. Using a small knife, carve an image while holding the wax block in one hand. Be careful to whittle small thin slices slowly. Continue this process until the desired image is realized.

Evaluation: Based on three-dimensional effects in the round.

LESSON 288   Balsa Wood Carving   Beginning/Intermediate/Advanced

Purpose: To carve a three-dimensional form from soft wood material.

Materials: Balsa wood blocks, beautician's razor blade or penknife, pencils, drawing paper.

Procedure: Have students work from a preliminary sketch. Redraw the sketch on a block of balsa wood, considering all four sides of the wood. Using a sharp razor blade or penknife, grasp wood in hand and whittle small segments carefully until the image begins to emerge. Carve as little as possible to identify the inherent image.

Evaluation: Based on simplicity of design and suitability of idea.

LESSON 289   Palette Knife Painting   Intermediate/Advanced

Purpose: To explore and use the versatile palette-knife technique in painting.

Materials: Masonite or heavy white cardboard, tempera paint, palette knife, pencils, drawing paper.

Procedure: After a preliminary drawing is made, have students redraw the composition onto masonite or heavy white cardboard. Masonite should be gessoed first. Using palette knife, apply tempera paint directly from can or squeeze bottle to the surface of the paper. Paint should be thick rather than thin. Move the paint around the surface of the composition by scraping rather than laying it on. Several effects can be gained by scraping, using edge of knife, and by using the flat of the knife with pressure. Paint will dry quickly, so mixing of color demands application before the first color is dry on the surface. Undesired colors can be scraped off. This technique is best used on open areas such as sky, land, and water. Accents are made with edge of the knife. Avoid details.

Evaluation: Based on effectiveness of knife technique, and total composition.

LESSON 290   Soft Brick Carving   Intermediate/Advanced

Purpose: To carve an image from a three-dimensional block of material.

Materials: Soft bricks, paring knives, saw blades, pencils, drawing paper, glue.

Procedure: Using a soft brick shape, have students work from a preliminary sketch. First cut or chip away excess brick. Saw or carve with paring knife the image being expressed. After all excess brick is carved away, add details with point of knife. Be careful of chipping. If this happens, replace with glue.

Evaluation: Based on roundness or three-dimensional effect as viewed from all angles.

LESSON 291   Alabaster Stone Carving   Intermediate/Advanced

Purpose: To execute a three-dimensional head or animal in alabaster.

Materials: Alabaster stone block, saw blades, paring knives, pencils, drawing paper.

Procedure: Have students prepare a preliminary sketch. Working from the sketch, saw or chip away small pieces of material until the suggested idea emerges. Then work slowly in dealing with details and recessive inner areas by using sharp narrow tools. Keep carving simple. Texture can be added as a final touch.

Evaluation: Based entirely on three-dimensional appearance from all angles.

LESSON 292   Simple Thumb Pot   Beginning/Intermediate/Advanced

Purpose: To model a pot from the most simple means.

Materials: Prepared clay, simple clay tools.

Procedure: Have students roll clay into a ball about the size of a tennis ball. While holding clay in one hand, push the thumb of the opposite hand down into the center of the clay ball. The clay should be squeezed between the thumb and fingers, rotating the clay with the fingers. Press the thumb deeper, rotating and squeezing at the same time. As this process continues, the walls and base should get thinner as the pot gets bigger. When the pot feels comfortable in the hand, the process should stop. Smooth out the inner and outer surfaces. Add desired textures with simple tools.

Evaluation: Based on the simplicity and roundness of form.

LESSON 293   **Linoleum Inlay**   **Intermediate/Advanced**

Purpose: To execute an inlay expression.

Materials: Wood panel or board, craft knife, large slab of linoleum, glue, pencils, linoleum cutters, cellulose filler, palette knife.

Procedure: Have students select a large piece of linoleum and glue it onto a wood panel. Draw a design or sketch onto the linoleum with a white or black pencil. Using linoleum cutters, gouge out the lines of the design in varying thicknesses. Then mix cellulose filler and work it into the cuts with a palette knife until all cut lines are filled. Allow to dry, then wipe clean.

Evaluation: Based on the total composition, considering variety of line cuts.

LESSON 294   **String Weaving**   **Beginning/Intermediate/Advanced**

Purpose: To execute a simple weaving technique.

Materials: Stout cardboard, string, needle, scissors.

Procedure: Have students wrap string around a stiff piece of cardboard to make a simple warp, first notching the cardboard at the top and bottom. Using a weaving needle, weave different types of string into the warp to form a design or pattern. After the weave is complete, cut across the unwoven side and knot the warp ends securely to each other in pairs. Finally, trim the ends if necessary.

Evaluation: Based on the consistency of design.

LESSON 295   **String Embroidery**   **Beginning/Intermediate/Advanced**

Purpose: To execute a simple technique of string design.

Materials: Burlap, stiff cardboard, staple gun, thread, needle, string.

Procedure: Have students stretch a piece of burlap over a piece of stiff cardboard and staple it down securely on the back. Stitch several kinds of string into the design of the burlap, in small segments or areas. Be sure to show a contrast between the string and the burlap. Use many different types and colors of string to create variations in the design.

Evaluation: Based on the variety within the design and the total composition.

LESSON 296   **Papier-Mâché Balloon-Model Head**   **Intermediate/Advanced**

Purpose: To use the balloon technique for papier-mâché portrait.

Materials: Various shapes of balloons, string, papier-mâché solution, newspaper strips, tempera paint, brushes, paint trays, water cups.

Procedure: Have students select the size and shape of balloon suitable to the type of head to be made. Have the balloon blown up and tied tightly with string. After strips of newspaper are soaked in papier-mâché solution, apply strips carefully over the entire balloon shape. Allow to dry. Prick the balloon and pull the remains out from the neck of the papier-mâché shape. Using the papier-mâché method, add facial features to the oval shape until complete. Paint the entire shape of the head to achieve a desirable effect.

Evaluation: Based on the personality of the portrait head as well as adherence to three-dimensional principles.

LESSON 297   **Metal Scrap Construction**   **Intermediate/Advanced**

Purpose: To arrange and compose metal scraps in a three-dimensional expression.

Materials: Metal scraps, solder, soldering iron, glue, wood base.

Procedure: Have students select various sizes and shapes of scrap metal. Working from a wooden base, attach pieces of metal to one another by soldering them in place. Always consider the weight of each piece before soldering. Continue this process until all pieces are soldered in place. Finally, attach to wooden base or allow to hang as a free form.

Evaluation: Based on the variety of sizes and shapes, and total balanced composition.

LESSON 298   **Plasticine Modeling**   **Beginning/Intermediate/Advanced**

Purpose: To model a figure or animal form from the simple medium of Plasticine.

Materials: Plasticine, simple modeling tools.

Procedure: Using the flexible material of Plasticine, have students model a complete figure, head, or animal shape. It would be helpful to make a preliminary sketch or to work from a visual stimulus. After work is complete, add details and textures as desired.

Evaluation: Based on the three-dimensional effects of the expression.

LESSON 299   **Plastics Construction**   Intermediate/Advanced

Purpose: To construct a three-dimensional project out of plastic scraps.

Materials: Plastic scraps, glue, wood base, finishing nails.

Procedure: Have students break larger sections of plastic pieces into small pieces. Glue pieces together in an upward and outward direction. The completed form can be used in a standing, hanging, or projecting position. Attach it to a wood panel if used as a stabile or wall plaque.

Evaluation: Based on effectiveness of three-dimensional principles.

LESSON 300   **Stone Painting**   Beginning/Intermediate/Advanced

Purpose: To apply a painted medium over a natural object.

Materials: Various types and sizes of stones, tempera paint, brushes, water cups, paint trays, fixative.

Procedure: Have students select a stone with texture, size, and shape suitable to the idea being expressed. Cupping stone in hand, apply paint to meet the shape and size of the stone. In other words, the stone should dictate the idea to be painted. After the stone is completely painted on one or both sides, allow to dry. Spray fixative over the stone for permanency.

Evaluation: Based on the unique application of the idea to the contour and texture of the stone.